A Guidebook for Cooperative Learning:

A Technique for Creating More Effective Schools

Dee Dishon

Pat Wilson O'Leary

Foreword By
David W. Johnson
Roger T. Johnson

LEARNING PUBLICATIONS, INC.
Holmes Beach, Florida

Dishon, Dee.
  A Guidebook for Cooperative Learning.

  Bibliography: p.
  Includes index.
  1. Group work in education. I. O'Leary, Pat Wilson,
1948-   . II. Title.
LB1032.D53 1984   371.3'95   83-83183
  ISBN 0-918452-58-9

Learning Publications, Inc.
P.O. Box 1326
Holmes Beach, Florida 33509

Cover Design: Barbara J. Wirtz

Printing: 1 2 3 4 5 6 7 8 Year 4 5 6 7 8 9

Printed and bound in the United States of America

Acknowledgments

We wish to thank all of those who have been our teachers as we have worked with cooperative learning: David Johnson and Roger Johnson, from whom we first learned about cooperative learning; Pat Roy, who added much practical information to the model; the teachers who taught us about cooperative groups by using them in their classrooms; and the workshop participants who kept saying, "Please write this down!"

We also wish to express appreciation to our places of employment* which gave us the opportunity to train ourselves and others. In working with teachers in workshop and classroom settings we have gained invaluable insight and skills.

Thanks also go to Chick Moorman for his suggestions and to Art O'Leary for his assistance with the graphics. We appreciate their continued support and encouragement.

* (Region 12 S.A.P.E.—Calhoun Intermediate School District and Kalamazoo Valley Intermediate School District)

*We dedicate this book to all
who believe that cooperation
is our basic skill for survival.*

Table of Contents

Foreword

This is a useful and exciting book by Dee Dishon and Pat Wilson O'Leary. For years, we have known them, worked with them, and admired their ability to develop practical classroom materials for structuring cooperative learning. They have a talent for translating important theoretical material and research findings into step-by-step procedures for teachers to implement in their classrooms. This book is a fine example of their talent.

Education is in a position where current educational practice contradicts what we know about effective instruction. While interpersonal competition and individualistic learning are being emphasized in most schools, there is considerable evidence that under most conditions instruction would be more effective if students worked in cooperative learning groups. This is true when schools wish to emphasize achievement and higher level reasoning processes, and it is true when schools wish to emphasize cognitive and social development.

Historically, there has been an emphasis on cooperative learning in our schools. Francis Parker and John Dewey are two of the most famous educators who implemented cooperative learning in schools. Throughout the United States there have always been teachers who structured lessons so that students collaborated in completing their assignments. Dee Dishon and Pat Wilson O'Leary are two of the educators whose roots extend back to the theorizing of Kurt Lewin and Morton Deutsch and whose practical application of cooperative learning has a heritage extending into the 1980's and beyond.

For the past 30 years, however, schools have been dominated by interpersonal competition and individualistic learning procedures. Students have been encouraged to work alone, ignore and try to out-perform each other. The pendulum is now swinging back into balance. Tens-of-thousands of teachers throughout North America are now beginning to utilize cooperative learning strategies in their classrooms. The evidence that cooperative learning, when compared with competitive and individualistic learning, results in higher achievement, greater achievement motivation, more positive attitudes toward learning, more constructive relationships among students even when students vary in ethnic background and achievement levels, higher level reasoning processes, higher self-esteem, and greater interpersonal competencies, is no longer being ignored. This does not mean that it is easy to implement cooperative learning. Most students are unskilled in collaborating and need specific training in how to work effectively with other students. Careful planning and considerable experience are needed for teachers to be able to use cooperation routinely in their classrooms. Teachers who are using cooperative learning strategies, and those teachers who are interested in beginning to do so, will find this book invaluable.

Structuring learning situations so that students invest themselves in each other's learning requires serious and committed efforts by teachers. Strategies for building positive interdependence ("sink or swim together") among students and for teaching collaborative skills, are being emphasized in many different subject areas and age groups. Dee and Pat are at the forefront of this training. In their work with school districts, they have taught demonstration lessons, observed teachers trying out cooperative learning, helped plan lessons for teachers to implement, provided one-on-one consulting help, and taught inservice and preservice courses on how to structure cooperative learning situations effectively. During their work they have developed practical procedures and materials that have proved very valuable to educators who wished to implement cooperative learning. After several years of encouragement to publish their materials to make them available to a wide range of teachers and educators, they have done so in this book.

Structuring cooperative learning activities, rather than competitive or individualistic ones, is a relatively simple idea. Implementing cooperative learning takes time, but the results are well worth it. Actually achieving the transformation from a competitive or individualistic classroom and school to a cooperative one, however, is difficult and takes perseverance as well as good ideas and effective strategies. Interested teachers will need support from each other and from their administrators. Interested teachers also need supportive materials and procedures to make the transition easier and more efficient. Dee and Pat have provided such support in this book.

David W. Johnson
University of Minnesota

Roger T. Johnson
University of Minnesota

Section I
Definition of Cooperative Groups

1
Introduction to Cooperative Learning

A major effort in education today seeks to create effective schools through implementation of a *cooperative learning model*. Educators who use this research-based model will put into practice an effective method of instruction for teaching academics and social skills, as well as democratic values.

The specific steps outlined in this guide are grounded in educational research. They are based upon recent evidence which indicates that, under most conditions, instruction is more effective when students work in cooperative learning groups rather than in situations where competition and individualistic learning are emphasized.

Cooperative learning, as presented here, is a model for teachers to use to teach the skills necessary for effective group work. Cooperative learning is a systematic model for helping teachers implement and work with groups so that students will consistently:

- Learn their subject matter
- Complete tasks
- Include all group members in their work
- Solve group problems with minimal teacher assistance
- Resolve differences among themselves
- Enjoy the process of working together

Cooperative learning procedures are appropriate for all levels and content areas—from pre-school through graduate school. These procedures help students practice skills and explore concepts which are a part of the established curriculum for their grade and subject area.

Students who work in cooperative groups learn important social skills which facilitate cooperation. With these skills, students relate appropriately to others who are different from them in terms of social background, physical condition, intellectual skill, or social proficiency. Research shows that the consistent use of cooperative teaching methods in the classroom helps students to learn and to care about others. Students learn to not only tolerate individual differences, but to value them as well.

In cooperative learning situations, students work and learn in groups. Of course, students working in groups is not new. Teachers have been using group methods for as long as there have been classrooms. None the less, many teachers tend to de-emphasize the use of groups because they have experienced group work in school settings to be disruptive and unproductive. This has resulted in their disillusionment with special group approaches to instruction. Furthermore, while most teachers recognize the value of cooperation and the benefits of students learning from each other, many allow their past frustrations to decrease their willingness to plan cooperative learning experiences.

In addition, some teachers mistakenly believe that particular personalities in their classrooms totally determine the outcome of special group work, regardless of how they organize group work. Of course, what the teacher does and does not do is critical to what students learn. There is nothing mystical about what enables teachers to successfully foster cooperative learning. We believe that the teacher's success depends upon the use of specific skills which can be taught and learned. There are skills which a teacher needs to know and skills which students must learn in order to work cooperatively with their peers. Without these student and teacher skills, group work will not be consistently successful and will require excessive teacher supervision.

How do you as a teacher acquire the skills needed for implementing cooperative learning? Knowledge and practice are needed. Knowledge of the required skills and how to teach these skills to students, combined with practice, will enable you to become proficient in facilitating cooperative learning experiences. This guidebook, implemented with your enthusiasm, determination and humor, will help you acquire the necessary knowledge and structure for practicing cooperative learning. You will then be able to teach your students to work productively and enjoyably in groups while achieving both academic and social goals.

Cooperative Learning In Action

Cooperative groups are different from typical classroom groups in several significant ways. These differences are illustrated through a visit to a fifth grade classroom where successful cooperative learning experiences occur. There are five important principles which underlie successful cooperative learning experiences. They are: The Principle of Distributed Leadership; The Principle of Heterogeneous Grouping; The Principle of Positive Interdependence, The Principle of Social Skill Acquisition; and The Principle of Group Autonomy. The five principles are outlined, illustrated and then followed by a discussion of how to put them into effect. You will then have an opportunity to examine how your beliefs and behaviors match those necessary for successful implementation of cooperative learning experiences.

Mr. Jordan's Class: An Illustration

As Walter Jordan's 32 fifth graders settle down after lunch, he asks for attention and announces that today's spelling lesson will be done in cooperative groups. Several students quickly ask, "Which groups are we in today, Mr. Jordan?"

"We'll number off for new groups after I give all of the directions," he explains. "Your group's job today is to practice your ten spelling words and make sure that everyone in your group can spell them. You will each get two of the ten words to learn and teach to the other people in your group. After 15 minutes of practice time, you will receive five of the ten words to spell correctly. Your group will help you during the practice time. During the test you're each on your own. Your group's score will depend on your results as a group, since your five scores will be added together."

Mr. Jordan writes the criteria on the board as he explains them.

90% — 100% = No one in your group has to take the test again

89% or less = Everyone in your group takes the test again

"Everyone in the class will get an extra ten minutes of recess tomorrow if the room score is 90% or better." There is a buzz of excitement about that possibility.

One child asks, "What are the social skills we practice today?" In response, Mr. Jordan tapes up one sheet of paper that is filled with writing. It is labeled "Check for Understanding."

"As you know, this is a social skill we practiced in math last week. Let's refresh our memories about what this social skill looks like and sounds like." He calls on individuals as they read or recall the words written on the sheet entitled "Check for Understanding." The class responds:

"Denise, will you spell this word?"

"Will someone check me on these?"

"Looking at the word that someone has written."

"OK, I think we're clear on that. Let's look at a new social skill today. This is one that some of you know. Today you are all to practice encouraging others while your group works on learning the spelling words." Pointing to a sheet labeled "Encourage Others," Mr. Jordan asks: "What can 'Encourage Others' sound like?"

"It's like a cheerleader."

"You can say 'Nice job!' or 'Way to go!'"

"How about 'We can do it!'?"

"Clapping and cheering."

Mr. Jordan records the students' words with a smile and a nod for each. "What can 'Encourage Others' look like?" he asks. His students give a variety of answers:

"A smile."

"A nod."

"A pat on the back."

"All right, you've definitely got the idea! Today I will observe each group. I will use an observation sheet to record how many times I see or hear you each using these social skills. I won't be observing your group for the whole time, but I want each of you to practice even when I'm not there."

"If you have any questions while I am busy observing, check with your group first for the answer. I will only answer one question per group, so make sure that it's a really important one. Now number off by 6's to see who is in which group."

When everyone has a number, Mr. Jordan points out where the groups are to sit. The groups quickly form. Three groups choose to be in a circle on the floor, two put chairs around two desks, one group forms around a small table. The random selection process has produced heterogeneous groups.

Mr. Jordan waits until all groups are settled before passing out two spelling words to each student. He moves from one group to the next, spending two to three minutes making tally marks on each group's observation form. He makes a mark under "Checking" beside Jim's name when Jim looks at a spelling word Carla has just written and says, "That's right."

After a few minutes of work time, Group #3 appears to be having trouble. Susan's chair is pushed far away from the group; her arms are folded and her face is stern. The teacher looks over at the group but makes no move towards them until three of the students raise their hands. Mr. Jordan promptly leaves the group he is observing and approaches them.

"Yes."

"Mr. Jordan, Susan won't share her words or practice the others. She says she hopes we all have to take the test again," Tracy explains.
"Well, your group certainly has a problem. What have you done so far to encourage Susan to participate?"

The group members glance at each other and back at their teacher. "We told her she'd better do it or we would tell you," Jason offers.

"I would like you to figure out three more ways to help invite Susan to join in with the group. I'll be back in a few minutes to see what your group has to report."

Walter then moves slowly around the room, continuing to mark the observation sheets. He returns to Group #3 in a few minutes with a question. "What does your group have to report?"

"We decided that we can ask her to leave; we can ask her to please help us out; or we can offer to help her learn her words," Tracy says. Susan has unfolded her arms and appears to be following the conversation.

"See which one appeals to Susan," says Mr. Jordan. "Susan, you move closer to the group and listen to each suggestion. I want you to all work this out together. I'll be back soon to see what you've decided."

The teacher walks away and doesn't look over until he returns to the group several minutes later. "What has your group decided?"

"We asked her to leave and do it alone if she doesn't want to help, but she said that she would rather stay in the group," says a group member.

"How is that with you, Susan?" asks Mr. Jordan.

"OK, I'll do it," says Susan.

"Fine," says Mr. Jordan. "Your group has just a little time left."

Five minutes later, Mr. Jordan calls a halt to work time and instructs students to rearrange their seats so that they're all separated from one another and facing toward the front of the classroom. It is time for the individual spelling test.

After the test, students correct their words. Groups move back together to compare and combine scores. The grading scale is on the board and students refer to it as they put their group's score on each of the papers. As Mr. Jordan walks around to each group, it is clear that Susan's group will have to take the test again. He stops at their group and asks, "How is your group going to do better on spelling next time?'' The group huddles for a moment before Tracy announces, ''We're all going to get to work sooner next time so we all learn our words.''

''Yes, we're all taking the words home to study for tomorrow's test,'' chimes in Kevin.

Mr. Jordan nods and smiles. ''We'll see how you do tomorrow. I know your group can do better.''

Calling the class to order, Mr. Jordan states, ''Now let's see how you did as a class on the test.'' He picks up each group's paper and quickly figures the room score. There is much cheering and applauding when he announces that the room score is above the previously stated criterion. Now there will be ten minutes of extra recess for everyone.

Although spelling papers have been checked, it is clear that neither the class nor the assignment is complete. Calling on individuals randomly, Walter inquires about various methods for learning spelling words. The class has many suggestions:

''By repeating them out loud all together.''

''By writing them several times.''

''I learned that some people have to hear a word a lot to learn it.''

There is a general consensus that:

- there are similarities and differences in methods that people use to learn spelling words; and

- whatever method works for each person is appropriate.

Mr. Jordan continues, ''Now let's look at how all the groups did on social skills. I want all of you, as a group, to copy and complete these two statements on the board. Use your own ideas about how you did on the social skills. Choose a person to record these ideas and then report them to the group.''

****
(To be written on the board or chart paper)

Analyze: Our group did best on _____
                                                    (social skill)

by: _____ ,

_____ ,   and

_____ .

(three specific behaviors)

Goal Setting: The social skill we will practice more often tomorrow is _____

_____ .

We will do this by (three specific behaviors): _____

_____ ,

_____ ,   and

_____ .

****

Mr. Jordan gives the class five minutes of group work to complete this task. During this time, he walks slowly around the room listening in on groups but not commenting. He calls the class to order and says, ''Please listen as each spokesperson reads his or her group's processing answers. Pay attention to any items that are alike or different from what your group recorded.''

As the spokespersons report, Mr. Jordan writes up any new behaviors as well as the goal which each group has set. When all reports are in he asks, ''What are some of the similarities and differences in the behaviors mentioned?'' Several responses are forthcoming and posted to be looked over before tomorrow's lesson.

Mr. Jordan then delivers the completed observation sheets to each group so that students can see how closely the data agrees with their conclusions. Only one group notices a discrepancy. Mr. Jordan noticed ''encouraging'' more than ''checking,'' and the group thought that they did best on checking. The group decides that it is because they happened to be doing more encouraging when Mr. Jordan was there. He just did not see all of the checking. Mr. Jordan agrees with their analysis, as he stops by their group.

''We're finished with this lesson today,'' Mr. Jordan announces. ''Tomorrow we will have a re-take of the test, plus there will be a spelling crossword puzzle for your group to solve. Now let's clean up and get ready to go to music class.''

Desks and chairs are quickly rearranged and the room soon resembles its earlier state. Recorders put the observer's form and written responses to the processing in a file folder which is then placed in a box on top of the filing cabinet. Cooperative learning time is over, but the cooperative spirit obviously remains.

The Five Underlying Principles

Does Mr. Jordan's cooperative group experience seem too good to be true? It is not. This is not Mr. Jordan's first experience with cooperative groups. It is almost Christmas. He has had three months in which to teach and practice cooperative learning skills with his students. What occurred in Mr. Jordan's classroom was not an accident nor a happy twist of fate. Mr. Jordan's students have learned specific social skills in a classroom environment which is based upon five important principles.

1. The Principle of Distributed Leadership
2. The Principle of Heterogeneous Grouping
3. The Principle of Positive Interdependence

4. The Principle of Social Skills Acquisition
5. The Principle of Group Autonomy

Each principle involves specific teacher behaviors which in turn can produce the desired result—student groups which demonstrate and benefit from cooperative learning skills.

1. The Principle of Distributed Leadership

Cooperative learning is based upon the belief that all students are capable of understanding, learning and performing leadership tasks. Experience and research show that when all group members are expected to be involved and are given leadership responsibilities, we increase the likelihood that each member will be an active participant who is able to initiate leadership when appropriate.

Teacher Behavior: No leader is assigned by the teacher or chosen by the group.

Example: Mr. Jordan neither assigned group leaders in his class nor did he tell each group to choose their leader.

2. The Principle of Heterogeneous Grouping

Cooperative learning is based upon a belief that the most effective student groups are those which are heterogeneous. Groups which include students who have different social backgrounds, skill levels, physical capabilities and genders mirror the real world of encountering, accepting, appreciating and celebrating differences.

Teacher Behavior: To insure hetereogeneity, the selection of groups is done randomly or group members are chosen by the teacher.

Example: The fifth graders in Mr. Jordan's class numbered off to be in randomly selected heterogeneous groups.

3. The Principle of Positive Interdependence

Cooperative learning is based upon a belief that students need to learn to recognize and value their dependence upon one another. Students who have had lots of practice working individually to complete their assignments or competitively to do better than their peers are often not initially eager to work with others. Incorporating positive interdependence increases the likelihood that students will work cooperatively.

Teacher Behavior: Positive interdependence is created when the teacher employs one or more of the strategies listed below.

• Group members are given common subject matter tasks.

• Group accountability is established.

- Individual accountability is established.

- Materials must be shared.

- Group members create *one* group product.

- There is a group reward which each group can earn and which is the same for all group members.

Example: In Walter Jordan's class positive interdependence was created in the ways listed below:

- The group's common task was for everyone to learn the spelling words.

- Each person was held accountable for knowing the material.

- Materials were "jigsawed" so that no one had all the words.

- The group score was based upon each individual's score.

- The reward is that no one has to retake the test if the group reaches criterion.

4. The Principle of Social Skills Acquisition

Cooperative learning is based upon a belief that the ability to work effectively in a group is determined by the acquisition of specific social skills. These social skills can be taught and can be learned.

Teacher Behavior: A teacher can teach specific cooperative social skills by defining, discussing, observing and processing with the students. In Chapters 5, 6 and 7 we will outline this procedure in step-by-step detail.

Example: In Mr. Jordan's fifth grade class we observed him using these techniques when:

- Previously used social skills were recalled with "looks like" and "sounds like" behaviors;

- New skills were defined and discussed;

- Social skills were practiced and observed; and

- Group members processed the lesson by analyzing group behavior and by setting goals for the next session.

5. The Principle of Group Autonomy

Cooperative learning is based upon the belief that student groups are more likely to attempt resolution of their problems if they are not ''rescued'' from these problems by their teacher. When students resolve their problems with a minimum of teacher input, they become more autonomous and self-sufficient.

Teacher Behavior: Typically, because we are members of a helping profession, we intervene to help students. We try to convince them to finish a task; we settle their arguments; and we offer *our* solutions to *their* problems. As a result, we deny students the opportunity to learn from failure and from each other. In addition, we often overload ourselves as teachers to the point of exasperation or ''burnout.''

Unless a group oversteps the boundaries of acceptable behavior or makes a group decision to solicit teacher assistance, it is more helpful for a teacher to suggest and prompt rather than direct student activity. The teacher's role should be as observer and monitor.

Example: Mr. Jordan removed himself from direct participation in the group work. While he encouraged Susan's group to explore solutions, he did not intervene with solutions of his own.

Needs Assessment

So far, we have examined a number of important principles and practices. We have illustrated them with Mr. Jordan's effective use of groups. You have seen the benefits of the procedures and the process. Also, you have been introduced to the five basic principles which make cooperative groups different from typical classroom groups. We now invite you to begin gathering data for needs assessment. What do you believe about group leaders and group membership? What behaviors do you exhibit when working with groups? What modifications would you like to make? Please continue by completing the following Belief/Behavior Inventory.

Belief/Behavior Inventory

1. Put an N (meaning ''Now'') in the ME column on the side that represents your present beliefs and behaviors.

PRINCIPLE #1 Distributed Leadership			
Cooperative Groups	Me		Typical Classroom Groups
Belief: All group members are capable of understanding, learning and performing the tasks required for a group to complete a task and like each other when the task is done.			Belief: One group member, chosen by the teacher or the group, is responsible for seeing that the task is completed and everyone likes each other when the job is done.
Behavior: No leader is assigned or chosen. All group members perform the leadership skills when appropriate.			Behavior: One leader is assigned or chosen. That leader performs all leadership skills or assigns them to group members.

PRINCIPLE #2 Heterogeneous Grouping		
Cooperative Groups	Me	Typical Classroom Groups
Belief: The most effective groups are heterogeneous in terms of social background, skill levels, physical capabilities and gender.		Belief: The most effective groups are homogeneous in terms of social background, skill levels, physical capabilities and gender.
Behavior: Selection of groups is made randomly or by the teacher to insure heterogeneity.		Behavior: The teacher selects groups based on similarities of group members.

PRINCIPLE #3 Positive Interdependence		
Cooperative Groups	Me	Typical Classroom Groups
Belief: All students are not willing to work in groups unless there is a built-in reason to do so.		Belief: Students will work together by being told to cooperate.
Behavior: There is a group product, group or individual accountability, shared materials, and/or group reward.		Behavior: Group members create one or more products, sometimes share materials, are accountable only for their own learning, and have individual rewards.

PRINCIPLE #4 Social Skills Acquisition		
Cooperative Groups	Me	Typical Classroom Groups
Belief: The ability to work effectively in a group comes from skills that can be taught and learned.		Belief: Students come to school knowing how to get along and work in groups.
Behavior: Social skills are defined, discussed, practiced, observed, and processed.		Behavior: Groups are told to cooperate.

PRINCIPLE #5 Group Autonomy			
Cooperative Groups	Me		Typical Classroom Groups
Belief: Students learn to solve their own problems by resolving them on their own rather than being rescued from them by the teacher.			Belief: Group members always need the teacher's help to solve problems.
Behavior: In problem situations, the teacher suggests and prompts at the request of the entire group.			Behavior: The teacher directs and orders groups to solve problems according to the teacher's observation.

2 . Analyze your position. If your N's are both on one side in each section, your beliefs are consistent with your behaviors. If your N's are not on the same side, you may experience stress because your beliefs and behaviors are inconsistent.

3 . Now think about where you would like to be in terms of your beliefs and behaviors. We are asking you to experiment with new behaviors when you use cooperative groups, so it will be helpful for you to examine your beliefs to see if they coincide with your new practices. Go back through the columns and put an F where you would like to be in the future.

4 . Look at each of the five sections again. Sometimes adjustments between beliefs and behaviors are necessary in order to avoid or reduce stress. Pick one marked with an F that you would most like to change and write an ''I'' statement here for yourself:

"From now on when I work with groups, my belief is:

_____

_____

so my behavior _____

_____

One way I can be sure to do this is to _____

_____ .''

Keep a record of your reactions as you read this book. As you notice ''ah-hahs'' or twinges, check back to this inventory and question yourself. Does the new information match your beliefs and behaviors? You can learn about your teaching self at the same time that you learn about cooperative groups.

Section II
Planning And Implementation Of Cooperative Groups

3

Planning Your First Lesson

Now that you have some information about cooperative groups and how they work, you must decide how you will implement cooperative learning in your classroom. What are the steps that will lead you to successful group experiences with your students? How do you begin planning for group work at your grade level or in your subject area?

In this section on planning and implementation, we lead you through what we call a "translation"—a process to help you change our model to fit your situation. We have developed a teacher-proven five-step planning process. This process provides for set-up, implementation, and processing of cooperative groups.

The Lesson Plan Worksheet which is provided in Appendix A and described in detail in this chapter will help to lessen the anxieties you and your students might experience as you attempt this new technique. Once cooperative groups become an integral part of your teaching repertoire, you will no longer need to complete the worksheet for each cooperative learning lesson.

Before developing your first lesson plan, select students who will be most receptive; the ones who are most likely to say, "You want us to cooperate? Okay!" Select a content area which is appropriate for your students, which will interest them and with which you feel comfortable.

Read the explanation for each step of the model lesson plan; read the examples which are given, and consider the suggestions offered. Then check the boxes and fill in the blanks. As you work through the five steps outlined in this chapter, you will be creating your first cooperative learning lesson plan.

Step 1
The Lesson

There are four parts to Step 1. The first part concerns choosing a lesson. We have two suggestions:

First, begin with an academic task. Often groups are used for meaningless or time-filler tasks. We want students to know that groups are appropriate for important work too.

Second, use skills which are familiar to your students. The tasks listed in the chart below have been used successfully with groups who are novices in terms of cooperative learning. These tasks require familiar skills and their successful completion has academic merit.

Primary

Match primary color cards with their names
Identify letters, sounds
Tell time
Recognize whole numbers and fractions
Match story titles with their main ideas
Review basal words
Memorize seasons, months, days of week
Sequence events
Check directions to and from given points
Identify animals, pictures and names
Add or subtract 2 and 3 digit numbers
Match cloud shapes with predictable weather

Intermediate

Study spelling, vocabulary
Practice math facts
Match states with capitals
Proofread paragraphs for punctuation to match given rules
Define and recognize synonyms, antonyms
Identify the area and volume of basic geometric shapes
Read a thermometer in Celsius
Identify continents, countries, states on maps
Label past, present, future tense of words
Name and label primary and secondary colors
Identify, name constellations
Alphabetize lists of words

Junior High/Middle School

Check math story problems
Identify parts of speech
Identify types of fabrics
Check measurements to properly follow a recipe
Match book categories to Dewey Decimal System
Label bones of the body
Match flags with states
Check ten sentences for correct punctuation
Write Roman Numerals 1 to 50
Identify all sections of the library
Know spelling and definitions of a list of homonyms

High School

Study spelling, vocabulary (for any content area)
Memorize the Periodic Table of Elements
Check geometric theorem proofs
Identify vocational machine parts and memorize safety rules
Label literary forms of six readings
Label samples of metaphor, simile
Match name with function of body organs
Identify reproductive parts of the flower
Match symbols with advertised products
Name the components of a short story
Check the computed costs of financing and running an automobile for one year
Match flags with countries of the world

You increase the possibility that this first cooperative group activity will be successful if you choose an academic skill that your students practice often. This also allows students to concentrate on the new group behaviors and social skills you will be assigning them to practice.

Step 1-A. Subject Matter Goal

Determine the outcome of your lesson. Check the appropriate box and fill in the short line with a brief description of the academic goal which will be clear to you and your students.

****

1-A. Outcome of the Lesson (general goal):

☐ To memorize _____

☐ To practice _____

> Is your statement clear to you? Will your students understand the objective of their assignment?

****

Step 1-B. Subject Matter Task

When choosing this first cooperative group task, assign an amount of work that can be completed during one class session and allows time for directions and processing as well. However, keep in mind that doing any assignment in a group will take longer than the same assignment which is done individually. If your students can do ten math problems individually during a twenty minute work period, they will probably be able to solve five problems in a group of three during the same amount of time. It takes more time in a group because members must spend time to:

- Check to see that everyone understands the assigned tasks

- Decide on a method to complete the task

- Give everyone a turn to complete part of the task

- Compare and agree upon answers

Be sure to clarify for students that this is a group task. Work is not to be done individually or competitively, but cooperatively.

Example: (The spelling lesson task which Mr. Jordan assigned in Chapter 2) ''Your group's job today is to practice your ten spelling words and make sure that everyone can spell them. You will each get two of the ten words to learn and to teach to the other people in your group.''

Look back at your general goal (1A) and write a task statement, in language that your students will understand, which specifically describes what students are to do in their cooperative groups. Divide the task into manageable steps if there are several parts.

****

1B. Subject Matter Task (specific objective):

"Your *group* will work cooperatively to:

1. _____   4. _____

2. _____   5. _____

3. _____   6. _____ "

Double check. When you write this subject matter task statement on the board, will everyone in the group know their part in the group assignment? Will everyone know the group task?

****

Step 1-C. Learning Experiences Which Precede Group Work

The third part of Step 1 is to determine what learning experience(s) will precede group work. As you begin to use cooperative groups, remember that you are going to continue to do whole class work and individual work as well.

Example: Mr. Jordan might have preceded his memorization lesson with a story containing the spelling words which students had read as a homework assignment, or an individual assignment for looking up the definitions of the spelling words, or a choral pronunciation of the spelling words by all class members.

Select from the three choices what learning experiences will precede this group lesson. Complete the description.

****

1C. Learning Experience(s) Which Precede Group Work:

☐ Lecture on _____

☐ Homework assignment on _____

☐ Lesson on _____

****

Step 1-D. Time Needed For Lesson

The fourth and final part of Step 1 is to plan how much time this particular lesson will take. Include time to give directions, work time for groups, correcting papers and discussing products, as well as processing. We recommend that you do your first lesson in one session. If you have high school students for 55 minutes or if you know that your third graders have an attention span of 30 minutes per activity, gauge your time accordingly. Below is a graph to help you visualize the time frame required.

Example for 60 Minute Period of Time

For now, plan enough time to begin and complete a successful cooperative group activity. How long will your lesson take? Fill in the blank.

****

1D.   Time for this one lesson is _____ minutes.

****

Step 2
Group Composition and Room Arrangement

How many students in a group, who is in which group, and how your room is arranged are all important management items to decide before group work begins. These decisions fall into several categories.

Step 2-A. Group Size

Begin with the size of your groups. Our recommendation is to start with groups of three. With a pair, we see a lot of nodding and smiling, and not much delving, discussion, or creative thinking. Groups larger than three require more time for work and processing. We have found that in a group of three, one person is likely to say, ''I don't get it'' or ask, ''Can you explain that?'' The uneven number of three encourages discussion and questioning and yet is small enough to get the task done in a reasonable amount of time.

For this first lesson, we recommend groups of three.

****

    2A. Group Size: <u>3</u>

****

Step 2-B. Teacher-Selected Heterogeneous Groups

Decide how you will choose who works in which groups. In the beginning we want you, the teacher, to have control of group composition. Randomly selected or student-selected groups do not insure the most powerful group dynamics. Studies show that students learn more academically and socially when the group members are different from rather than similar to one another. Student selection does not guarantee heterogeneity since students often select others just like themselves. Teacher-selected heterogeneous cooperative groups give students an opportunity to work with and appreciate people different from themselves.

How do you determine the mixture of differences in your groups? Research suggests that the strongest groups have students with a variety of skill levels, and we suggest that you use this as one criterion. If you want students to appreciate similarities and differences, create groups which mix general education and special education students, remedial and gifted students, boys and girls, or members of different races. Would you like shy students to speak out more and outgoing students to learn to listen to others? Mix those types in one group. You may choose more than one category, but do not be over zealous. You will have many future groups in which to mix students and achieve heterogeneity. Check one or more of the choices below.

****

    2B. Teacher-Selected Heterogeneous Groups. Criteria for selection: (choose 1 or 2)

        ☐ High/average/low skills in _____

        ☐ Handicapped/non-handicapped

        ☐ Male/female

        ☐ Racial

        ☐ Outgoing/shy

        ☐ _____

Below are spaces for the names of the group members you choose. Write the names, and then you are ready to move on to the next step.

Group 1	Group 2	Group 3	Group 4	Group 5
_____	_____	_____	_____	_____
_____	_____	_____	_____	_____
_____	_____	_____	_____	_____

Group 6	Group 7	Group 8	Group 9	Group 10
_____	_____	_____	_____	_____
_____	_____	_____	_____	_____
_____	_____	_____	_____	_____

****

Step 2-C. Room Arrangement

Desk and room arrangement are important factors in group productivity and in maintaining your sanity. The scraping of thirty desks across the room will not endear you to your colleagues and will not help strengthen your belief that groups are a pleasant part of your instructional repertoire. Deciding how you want the room to look when students are working in cooperative groups and how you will achieve that look are preplanning *musts*.

Consider the following:

1. Get group members close together. You do not want a large table creating distance between students. This activity is neither labor negotiations nor a royal dinner party. Use one desk and two chairs, one end of a table, chairs in a tight cluster, or have students sit in a circle on the floor. Group members must be working close together facing one another if they are to complete the subject matter task and practice social skills too.

2. Have all group members on the same level. If you and your students are comfortable doing so, students may sit on the floor. But *everyone* in these groups must be on the floor. It is not acceptable for some members of the group to be on the floor and others to be in chairs. In a cooperative group, everyone is equal; equal in place, position and power, as well as equal in opportunity to participate and learn.

3. Have clear access lanes between groups since you will be moving among them, and students may need to move to obtain classroom resources. Because group conversation is a must, some space between groups provides a noise buffer as well.

Picture your room and its furniture. Check a description that fits how you will physically arrange groups for this lesson.

****

2C.   Physical Setting for Students:

☐ _____ Chairs in a circle
☐ _____ Students on floor in circle
☐ _____ Desks with _____ chairs

****

Step 3
Positive Interdependence

Since not all students will automatically want to work with others in a cooperative group, you need to create a feeling of "We sink or swim together." This feeling is called positive interdependence. To facilitate a caring situation, the teacher creates extrinsic reasons for students to work together.

There are three ways to create positive interdependence. The teacher may control the distribution or amount of resources, structure forms of accountability, and/or offer rewards. We will examine the three parts of Step 3. Then you can choose one or more of the methods to use in your lesson plan.

Step 3-A. Resource Interdependence

The materials given to students can be "jigsawed" or limited. To jigsaw materials means that everyone in the group gets a part of the necessary materials and the group needs all of the parts to complete the group task.

Sharing limited resources is another way to create positive interdependence. Giving one paper and one pencil to a group helps draw group members together to complete an assignment. Limiting resources is important not only in light of budget constraints, but is also the best way to increase the chances that cooperation will occur within the group.

Decide how you will use resources to create positive interdependence by checking one of the boxes and filling in the description.

****

3 A . Resource Interdependence:

☐ Jigsawed (each group member has a different part of the work or materials)

☐ Limited (each group gets fewer materials than there are group members)

```
┌─────────────────────────────────────────────────────────┐
│  Materials                                                │
│                                                           │
│  Number Needed:        Description:                       │
│                                                           │
│  _____       _____          │
│                                                           │
│  _____       _____          │
│                                                           │
│  _____       _____          │
└─────────────────────────────────────────────────────────┘
```

****

Step 3-B. Accountability Interdependence

Accountability refers to the ways you check on task accomplishment or evaluate each group product. It is important to let students know prior to worktime just how they will be held accountable. You have several choices. Will the group have one paper to correct? Will you randomly call on one person to explain the group's work? Or will everyone be checked on individual work and the scores combined?

Example: In the 5th grade spelling lesson described in Chapter 2, everyone took an individual test and then scores were combined.

Accountability requires criteria for judgment. As you check for accountability, what standard will you use? Determine if you will hold students accountable for their work. What will be acceptable work and what will be unacceptable?

Look back to Chapter 2. In Mr. Jordan's class, a score of 90% or better was above criterion for the task assigned. For any group which achieved that score or better, no member had to retake the test. For any group that achieved 89% or less, everyone in the group had to retake the test.

Decide what accountability and criteria you will require for this lesson. Complete Step 3B.

****

3 B .   Accountability Interdependence (Teacher Evaluation of Group Work):

☐ Explanation of group's work from individual(s)

☐ Check the group's paper

☐ Individual test to each student

Criteria—standard for judgment

☐ Grades

☐ Percentages

___ = _____

___ = _____

___ = _____

___ = _____

___ = _____

****

Step 3C. Reward Interdependence

The third way to create positive interdependence deals with offering students rewards for meeting criteria.

There are basic rules to remember about rewards:

- If your students willingly work in groups, do not give a reward. We suggest a reward only if your students are reluctant group members.

- Everyone in the group gets the same reward or no one gets one. Each group has access to the reward so there is no competition between the groups. Use of rewards does not encourage cooperation if groups have to fight over a limited number of prizes.

- If a group does not reach the criterion and does not receive the reward, it is helpful if the reward is not so attractive that blood or tears will be shed. Giving the group a second opportunity to reach the criterion by rechecking the problems, retaking the test, or labeling the parts again are other options.

- Withdraw rewards as your students begin to willingly work together. (Reward interdependence will be discussed in greater detail in Chapter 8.)

Decide if you will give a reward for this lesson. If so, what will it be? (There are suggested rewards listed in Appendix G.) Write your decision below.

****

3C. Reward Interdependence (each person in the group gets the same one; reward is available to all groups):

☐ Group recognition of _____

☐ Special privilege of _____

☐ A tangible reward of _____

> Check back through the three parts of Step 3. Be sure that you have chosen one or more ways with which to create positive interdependence, the feeling of "We sink or swim together."

****

Step 4
Social Skills

Every cooperative group assignment has two major components, completion of the subject matter task and the practice of social skills. Social skills are divided into *task* and *maintenance skills*. Task skills are those needed to complete the assignment. Maintenance skills are those needed to maintain the group in working order. It is not sufficient that a group completes an academic assignment. To be a cooperative group, members must also practice the social skills that enable them to like, or at least tolerate, each other. In some classrooms where we have observed, toleration would be a pleasant change from the status quo.

We recommend that you choose no more than one task skill and one maintenance skill. Or that you choose only one social skill if you think that is all your students can handle.

At first, we recommend that you choose from these four basic social skills:

Task: ☐ Check for understanding

                ☐ Share ideas and information

Maintenance: ☐ Encourage

                ☐ Check for agreement

Descriptions of Social Skills

Check for Understanding. Use of this skill lets group members know who understands the work and who does not. It is also a way of including all group members in the decision-making process.

Share Ideas and Information. If everyone shares their ideas and information, everyone will be participating in the group, not letting someone else do the work. The ideas and information that are shared in the group increase the resources available for decision-making.

Encourage. In many classrooms there are more negative comments than positive comments among students. We suggest teaching the skill of "encouraging" to motivate students to participate and to increase positive comments between students.

Check for Agreement. It is important for this skill to be used to insure that the group product is the result of all group members agreeing to the answers, not just one person or part of the group doing the work. This checking also brings students into the group discussion when they agree or disagree with the group's work.

Look back to your content assignment, Step 1A & B, to help you choose social skills that complement your task. For example, if you ask students to agree on their answer, assign "Check for agreement" as a social skill. Now decide for this lesson.

****

4. Social Skills (choose 1 or 2):

Task: ☐ Check for understanding

                ☐ Share ideas and information

Maintenance: ☐ Encourage

                ☐ Check for agreement

****

Step 5
Processing

Processing is one of the basic differences between typical classroom groups and cooperative groups. It provides closure for an activity, increases the possibilities of transfer of knowledge, and provides students with another opportunity to discuss their learning experiences in their own words.

There are many ways to process. We will describe them in depth in Chapter 7. For now, choose from the given examples. Have students judge what they did to get the subject matter task done. Also have them consider their use of the social skills.

Notice that we wrote "students judge," "they discuss," and "students plan." It is crucial that students finish the processing statements. Their reactions are based on what they remember and perceive about what happened during group work. It is your job to choose the statements. It is not your job to complete them. You will have an opportunity to respond after students have processed. Guidelines for doing that are provided in Chapter 7.

Step 5-A. Subject Matter Processing

We assume that you and your students process subject matter assignments by the papers that are graded, the questions that are asked, and the class discussions that are held. The idea of processing subject matter is not new in classrooms. Since processing subject matter is valuable when done consistently, we encourage you to do so. Don't leave out this step because you are adding the processing of social skills. Choose one of the three statements to which students will respond.

****

5A. Subject Matter (Choose 1):

☐ Some ways we checked our facts are _____ ,

_____ , and _____ .

☐ One way we memorized _____ was to _____ .

☐ We   practiced _____ by _____ .

****

Step 5-B. Social Skills Processing

There are three different types of processing for social skills:

1. Analysis (Students judge how well they worked in this group *today*);
2. Application (Students discuss how to *transfer* the social skills learnings to other situations);
3. Goal setting (Students plan which social skill to work on the *next time* this group works together).

****

5B. Social Skills (Choose one type and one method):

☐ *Analysis* (examination of this group experience)

☐ Our group did well on _____
(social skill)

by _____ , _____ , & _____ .
(three behaviors)

☐ Continuums _____
Always   Never

We checked for understanding.   We encourage each other to participate.

We shared ideas and information.   We checked for agreement.

☐ *Application* (transfer of social skill learnings to other situations)

   ☐ We learned that in any group it is helpful to _____ .

   ☐ The social skill of _____ could be used at other times like _____

   _____ .

☐ Goal Setting (plans for next group session with same group members)

   ☐ The social skill we will use more next time is _____ because _____

   _____ .

   ☐ The social skill we will practice more next time is _____

   by _____ , _____

   and _____ . (three behaviors)

****

These initial decisions and planning may seem time consuming. However, you will find that they will facilitate the implementation of your first cooperative group lesson. Now that these decisions are made, the steps outlined in Chapter 4 will further help you to put your plans into action.

4

Lesson Plan Implementation

Students: "Where is Group 3? I can't find my group."

"You want me to work with *her*? No way!"

"Now what are we supposed to do?"

Teacher: "Okay, students, quiet down. Why is there so much commotion in your groups?"

Even the best plans can fail unless you consciously decide how to put your lesson plan into action. Careful pre-planning *plus* careful implementation increases the possibility of positive group experiences for you and your students. Our suggestions come with no guarantee, but many teachers find that implementing these steps increases the likelihood that group work will be effective and satisfying for you and your students.

We suggest that you read this chapter as you would a script. You may even want to follow it step-by-step for your first performance as a cooperative group facilitator. Notice that the presentation to students is in a slightly different order than the lesson plan outlined in Chapter 3. Explanations are arranged chronologically, according to whether they are given before, during, or after group work. Let's start by creating a "mindset" for cooperation.

Preparing Students for Cooperation

Because a focus on cooperation may be new to students, we suggest several ways to set the scene. When you begin using cooperative groups or introduce new skills, do one or more of the following activities:

- Start with a discussion of students' experiences with the assigned skill. For example, ask students when they have practiced encouragement with others. When have they been encouraged by others? How have they felt when someone took the time and effort to encourage them?

- Have students move into groups of two. Ask the partners to exchange ideas of how they might *encourage* (or any other social skill) each other in their group. Make a list of the words and non-verbal behaviors suggested by the class.

- Ask one group to be the actors in a role play. Have them come to the front of the room and practice the group assignment, using the social skills just discussed. The rest of the class watches. Afterwards, ask the class when and how the demonstration group used the social skills.*

---

*For ideas on introducing students to cooperation, see Gene Stanford, *Developing Effective Classroom Groups* (New York, NY: Hart Publishing Co., 1977).

Only a few minutes spent doing this preparation usually leads students to a better understanding of the need for the skills. Later, when defining the skill, point specifically how the skills are helpful in the cooperative group.

Your First Lesson

Before Group Work. What happens as soon as you put students into groups? Of course, *they talk.* Sometimes their talk is about the assignment; sometimes it is about totally unrelated topics. Whatever the topic, there are certain directions you will want to give students before they move into groups.

Subject Matter Objective (Step 1B). Write the subject matter objective on the chalk board (copied from your lesson plan, Step 1B), even if you teach young children who are non-readers. The written directions send the message, "This is important work." They also help older students to answer the question, "What do we do next?"

Read the subject matter objective aloud and briefly explain that group work is yet another way of learning in your classroom. Show the relationship between the subject matter content which will now be done in groups and previous content covered individually or in a whole class setting. (See Chapter 3, Step 1C for examples.)

Positive Interdependence (Step 3). It is crucial to create the feeling of "We sink or swim together" or there may be no motivation for students to work together. For this reason, students need to know the group rules for positive interdependence before they begin work. Share with students each choice that you have made in Step 3 of the lesson plan by writing each one on the board:

Resources (3A):

- What materials are assigned to each group

- Whether you will distribute materials or whether they will be available at a materials center

Accountability (3B):

- How group work will be evaluated

- The standard of judgment or criteria which will be used for evaluation

Reward (3C):

- What the reward will be

- How and when each group may obtain the reward

Sometimes teachers do not tell students about accountability and rewards until after the assignment has been completed. Afterwards is too late. These components of positive interdependence are sometimes the only reasons that students are encouraged to become actively involved in a group. Do not keep any of these reasons a secret.

Social Skills (Step 4). In the first lesson it is not enough to tell students the social skills and write them on the board. It is necessary to introduce social skills to students before you ask them to practice those social skills, just as you introduce math facts to students before you ask them to practice those math facts on their own. Spending time adequately preparing students to use social skills is time well spent. It is only necessary to do this introductory step once for each new skill; not each time the class does group work.

Take each social skill you have chosen and tell students whether the skill is a task or maintenance skill. Brainstorm with students about the specific behaviors "seen" and "heard" as each skill is practiced. We will discuss the social skill of "Encourage Others" as an example.

Write "Encourage Others" on chart paper. Then write the students' responses to the question "What does 'Encourage Others' look like and sound like?"

Encourage Others

Sounds Like	Looks Like
"We can do it. Let's go!"	Smile
"Keep after it. You are almost there."	Pat on back
"Good job!"	Nod
"Let's try it again."	Eye contact
	Leaning toward person

These are samples of how specific the behaviors must be in order to be effective and observable. We find that a minimum of six specific behaviors for each social skill is the most helpful. Notice, too, that we have included non-verbal as well as verbal behaviors, since messages are also sent through body language.

We suggest avoiding lists such as "What *Not* To Do in Groups" or "*Bad Things* For Group Members To Do." Putting these on display puts negative pictures in students' minds, rather than the positive images of what they are supposed to do to be helpful group members. It may be appropriate to briefly discuss unhelpful behaviors, but it is the helpful behaviors that are discussed at length, recorded, and put on display for later reference.

Follow the same procedure for each new social skill that is introduced. Keep these sheets and post them each time group work is done. This saves time and serves as a constant visual reminder of appropriate group behavior. These sheets can be referred to and added to each time students work in groups.

Having determined which academic task to complete and which social skills to practice, it is almost time to move students into groups and start them working. Remember, however, any other announcements should be made *before* you give the signal.

Post the names of group members before group work begins. This will reduce the noise and confusion.

List names on:

- A bulletin board, tag board, or chalk board; or on

- A sign posted near the location where each group will work.

Students may then check where and with whom they are supposed to work, without asking the teacher.

****

Decide where you will write group members' names, and record that here:

I will write group members' names on _____
                                                    (material)

and post the lists _____ .
                          (location)

****

It is common for students to react negatively to group assignments at first. Be firm in your choices and be prepared to respond to typical comments like:

Comment: "I want to work with my friends."

Suggested Response: "In this classroom, we work with more than our present friends. I want you to work with other people too."

Comment: "I don't want to work with *her* !"

Suggested Response: "This year we will work in many cooperative groups. At some point in time, you will work with everyone in this room."

****

Is there some other comment that you would like to be ready for? Write that comment and your response here:

Comment: _____

_____

Response: _____

_____

****

Our experience in watching successful cooperative group teachers is that it is best not to argue about who will work with whom and why, or to listen to complaints. The expectation is "You *will* work together," and that is what is done.

Room Arrangement (Step 2). Arranging the room the way you planned may go well or it may look and sound like the world at war. To avoid confusion, you may want to:

- Arrange the room before students come into the room (before school or at lunch time).

- Give specific location directions to groups ("Group 1, sit here by my desk; Group 2, sit by the book shelf; Group 3, sit by the closet," etc.)

- Write or draw a diagram for students to follow;

- Have students practice how to get up and move quietly; or

- Remind students that they need only to move themselves, not the furniture if you have not pre-arranged the desks.

****

Which methods will you use for this first lesson to get students into their groups? Write them here:

_____

_____

****

Announcements to Students. Before you begin to observe, announce to students how much time you will spend near each group. Probably two or three minutes will be your average amount of time. Be sure to tell students exactly what you are looking for, what you are recording, and that the data will be shared with each group.

You may want to tell students that you are "invisible." Make it clear that you are observing, and that you are not at each group to be an active member or to solve problems. (See Chapter 5 for more information about interacting and intervening.) If students need your help, they may ask a group question, one that each member in the group agrees they cannot answer for themselves.

Giving the Signal to Move. You have told students what they are to do for the academic and the social skills tasks. They have been told how they will be held accountable for their work. They know where or with whom they will be working. *Now* it is time to move students into groups. GO!

During Group Work. While students are in their groups working, there is an important task for you to perform. It is time for you to observe and monitor groups.

Teacher as Observer. Because social skills are so important to each cooperative group lesson, one of the teacher's most important jobs is to observe the students using the assigned social skills. There are two forms for recording data from which to choose—the individual form and a class form. Both forms are used for tallying the number of times you see and hear individual students practicing the prescribed social skills. When you use the individual form, you use a different form for each group. Shuffling those papers can be a challenge. However, later on you will have a single sheet of paper to return to the group.

Individual Group Form SKILLS	Susan	Paul	Cal	Kathy
Encourage				
Check for understanding				

The class form was designed by a teacher who did not want to shuffle observation sheets. After group work, the group data may be cut apart and handed to each group.

Both forms may have names and skills filled in even before students come into the room. This saves time and prevents confusion for you once groups start to work. (See Appendix B for blank forms.)

COOPERATIVE LEARNING
CLASS OBSERVATION FORM

LESSON: Social Studies

DATE: 9/15

GROUP#	NAMES	SOCIAL SKILLS	
		1. Check for understanding	2. Encourage
	Ed		
1	Rosa		
	Howard		
	Kim		
2	Sally		
	Joe		

Whether you use the individual group form or the class form, observe in the same manner. Make a tally each time you notice a social skill being used. You are near each group for only a few minutes. Remember that while many uses of the social skills will be tallied, some will be missed. Whatever data you are able to tally will be sufficient for groups to use in their processing.

Here are some guidelines to help you in your role as observer:

- Walk around to each group, spending only the few minutes scheduled.

- Listen and watch for students using the social skills.

- Mark a tally in the appropriate box on the observation form each time you see or hear an assigned social skill being used.

- Be alert for non-verbal behaviors, such as hand gestures, eye contact, body position, nodding.

- Observe what you can—you will not be able to see and record everything.

You might be surprised by some students. Sometimes they will exaggerate their use of social skills when you are observing their group. That is *good news*! We want students to practice, even over-exaggerate, as they try the skills. You might also notice students using the skill, but acting dull and lifeless. Eventually seemingly artificial or insincere practice can develop into conscious use of the social skills.

Teacher as Monitor. It is important that you monitor groups just as you promised before group work began. Be sure that you follow these guidelines:

- Keep to your observation schedule.

- Do not interrupt group work.

- Answer only group questions. To be sure, ask, "Is this a group question?"

This may be a different way of operating from what you are accustomed to doing. However, we urge you to do it anyway. Teacher attitude and action during group work is so important that we have an entire chapter which will provide you with more information and guidelines. (See Chapter 5, "The Teacher's Role During Group Work."

Work time will go quickly. Students will be practicing words or memorizing facts as well as performing their newly-learned social skills. You will be observing and monitoring groups as they work. When you end the session, tell students to remain in their groups.

After Group Work

Processing (Step 5). Every cooperative group lesson is processed. Students decide and judge how they handled the subject matter task and the social skills. To make these decisions, students have three resources:

1) Their perceptions of how and what they did in a group

2) The processing questions to which you ask them to respond

3) Observation sheet information

To help students use their resources, we suggest that you facilitate matters by following this prescribed procedure:

1. Write on the board the one subject matter processing selection you made in the lesson plan. (Step 5A)

2. Post the social skills processing selections. (Step 5B)

3. Give students a few minutes to discuss and decide what responses they will give to each processing statement. *They* will need to pick a spokesperson.

4. Return groups to a whole-class setting. The whole class listens as you record responses (as given or a paraphrase of lengthy ones) presented by the spokesperson.

5. Ask students to comment on the similarities and differences between responses.

6. Present each group with the observation sheet after the groups have discussed social skills.

7. Keep the following guidelines in mind as you make comments:

    *   Avoid judgmental terms like "excellent," or "poor."

    *   Avoid comparing groups or individuals.

    *   Use descriptive statements that start with phrases such as:

        "I noticed . . . "

        "I heard . . . "

        "I saw . . . "

8. Go back to the original social skills list of "looks like, sounds like." The following items may be added to the list:

    *   New ways you noticed students practicing the social skills

    *   New ways students noticed themselves practicing the social skills

    *   Learnings gained from processing

    These additions may be used as reminders during future cooperative group work.

The processing of social skills is now finished for this lesson and will have taken about ten or fifteen minutes of class time. You are probably asking yourself, "Is that time worthwhile?" Believe us, it is! Students begin to look at their own words and actions. For some it could be a new experience. With practice, students learn for themselves how to judge their behaviors. You set up the experience. They process the experience. Everyone in the class benefits.

You are done—almost. Before you close your plan book, take a couple of minutes to process how this lesson went for *you.*

****

What I liked best about this lesson was _____

_____ .

What I liked least about this lesson was _____

_____ .

What I will change next time I use this lesson is _____

_____

_____ .

****

We hope that your first cooperative lesson is the beginning of many group lessons which you will implement in your classroom. In this next section, the question of "How do I continue and vary cooperative groups?" will be answered.

Future Cooperative Group Lessons

To continue, we suggest that you explore new ways and times to use cooperative groups. Decide how to adapt group work to meet various students needs and classroom situations. Let's examine the flexibility which is available to you.

Choice of Class

You started with the class of least-resisters, the students who would be most willing to learn the cooperative learning process right along with you. We recommend that you continue using cooperative groups with that first class on a consistent basis. However, you will eventually want to move on to other classes and other subjects. The more you use cooperative groups and teach the social skills, the more you will be convinced that the method and the process are sound. Then you can promote it with the rest of your students. Continue to provide students with individual and competitive learning experiences for variety. Even with a method as successful as cooperative groups, moderation is a key factor.

Timing

To keep you and your students proficient in the use of cooperative skills, we recommend that you use groups at least twice a week with the same students. That way they can practice the social skills on a regular basis. If you attempt to use cooperative groups every day for every lesson, you and your students will tire of the method. Find the balance that works for you. Use groups often enough so that students say, "Can we do this assignment in cooperative groups?" but not so often that you hear, "Not groups again!"

When To Use Cooperative Groups

To reinforce the notion that important and challenging work can be accomplished in cooperative groups, we asked you to begin with lessons involving practice or memorization. Since there are many basic skills, you may continue with those short-term subject matter tasks. However, you may also want to add non-academic tasks. Teachers, experienced in using cooperative learning groups, have scheduled a variety of activities in cooperative groups. They include selecting the cast for the play, making an inventory of the lab equipment, or completing an art project. Many of the chores necessary in every room, at every level, may be turned into enjoyable activities, if done as a group.

Members of cooperative groups are also able to succeed in completing long-term projects. Lessons may be designed which take several class periods. Such projects include the planning of a field trip, writing a research report, painting a mural, and laying out the yearbook. The differences when doing long-term projects include: groups staying together until the projects are completed; lessons which are broken down into manageable steps which may be completed each time the groups meet; social skills which may vary with each meeting; and processing which is done after every session as well as at the end of the project. All of the steps for teaching social skills remain the same.

Use your imagination. Be creative. Soon you will be able to consider any activity and decide how to make it a cooperative group task. (See Appendix C for additional non-academic areas in which to use cooperative groups.)

Groups: Size, Selection and Longevity

Size. Group sizes range from a minimum of three students to a maximum of twelve. How do you decide the right number? First, look at the *skills* of the group members. If they are unskilled at working in groups, groups of three or four are appropriate. Highly skilled students may be able to work successfully in a group of twelve.

Second, consider the *amount of work* to be done. If the group is studying ten spelling words, three or four members would be adequate. If the task is to complete a report on Abraham Lincoln, the task could be successfully completed by eight or ten group members.

Third, figure the amount of *time* which is available. If you have a 45-minute class period or less, smaller groups are more appropriate to finish a small task. It could be, however, that cooperative groups may continue their work for several days for a short amount of time each day. The more time you have for groups, the larger each group may be.

Fourth, remember that the more people there are in a group, the more resources there are as well. This is good news and bad news. The good news is that the more people there are, the more ideas, information and opinions there are to help the group perform its task. However, the more people there are to hear from, the more time and effort it takes to get the job done.

Selection. It is a given fact that the most productive cooperative groups are heterogeneous. But it is not a given fact that groups must always be chosen by the teacher. Groups may be randomly chosen or chosen by students.

Random groups may be created by counting off; having every person wearing red in one group, green in another, etc.; or by drawing group numbers out of a hat. Student selected groups are also a possibility. However, we suggest that you wait to let students select their own groups until they have had several successful group experiences. Then, students will be more likely to choose people they would enjoy working with rather than on the basis of social ties. We also recommend that on the first few occasions during which you allow students to pick their own groups, that you do so for assignments that are not crucial. It takes an experience or two for students to realize that even when they have selected their groups they are still responsible for practicing the social skills and following all of the cooperative group rules.

Vary the way that groups are chosen in your classroom. If you always choose the groups, you send the message that only the groups that *you* set up will be successful. A more helpful message is that *any* group of students from your room can work together successfully in a cooperative group.

Longevity. Teachers often ask us, "How long should I keep groups together?" There is no right answer for that question. We have already given you many ideas for selecting group members and promoting the idea that everyone can work together. Of course it is okay to switch groups. A suggested "rule of thumb" is: Have students stay in groups long enough to complete the task; to create feelings of trust and respect; and to set and accomplish social skill goals. However, do not keep groups together so long that they see themselves as a team. That creates competition; team against team. As one of our teachers says, "When I see group members together in the hall, in the lunch room, in the library, I decide that they have been together too long. It is time to get students moving and comfortable with others in the classroom." Use your intuition and common sense. Move group members often enough for variety, but not so often that students feel that they are playing a game of Musical Chairs.

The most critical rule of all is to avoid breaking up a group when it is in trouble (disagreeing, not doing the work). That is definitely *not* the time to move group members. Have the group members resolve their problems to some acceptable standard before breaking up the group.

Differences Between and Among Groups

Believe it or not, there are lots of ways to vary cooperative groups. At first, we recommend that all groups work on the same task assignment and social skills. That makes giving directions easier. However, just as all students are not on the same level when doing independent and competitive work, they will not be on the same level when doing cooperative work. Provide a variety of experiences in response to these differences.

Assignment. Groups differ in their task assignment. Some groups move on to new skills and assignments, others need to review past academic assignments, and others still need to practice today's work.

With some groups, you might even have a variance within the group. A gifted student might have to learn to spell and define the week's vocabulary words; an average student might have to spell the vocabulary words; and your mainstreamed student might only have to recognize and pronounce the words. All of those tasks can be done in the same group. Everyone in that group is responsible for the others completing their assignments, even though their assignments are not the same.

Criteria. It might be appropriate for you to decide that students within a group have different criteria. In the above sample, the gifted student's criterion could be 90%; the average student's criterion, 80%; and the mainstreamed student's criterion, 75%. If everyone reaches criteria, they all get the same reward.

Setting. Not everyone in the room needs to be working in cooperative groups at the same time.

- You may work with a selected number of students while other students work in cooperative groups. On some days it might be necessary for you to have one-third or one-half of the class work with you in a directed-teaching situation. For example, a majority of the students need your attention to learn the next five items on the Periodic Chart of Elements. That means that members of the class who have mastered that task or who only need to review may work in cooperative groups to complete a lab experiment involving an element from the chart.

- You may facilitate one or two cooperative groups while the rest of the class works individually on a homework assignment.

- You may work individually with students on an assignment while one or two cooperative groups complete a project.

- You may work with a reading group in one part of the room doing a choral reading of basal words. The other students may work in cooperative groups or alone.

The variations are many. You do not have to mold your situation to fit some rigid concept of how to use cooperative groups. You may instead mold cooperative groups to fit your situation.

Steps to Teaching Social Skills*

There are innumerable ways to use cooperative groups. Apply them to your students, and adapt them to situations in your classroom. There is, however, *one* procedure that remains constant. That is the procedure for teaching social skills.

We will review the steps that you followed in your first cooperative group lesson. We recommend that you continue to implement these steps as you move ahead with cooperative learning experiences.

Step 1. Define and provide rationale for the skill.

Step 2. Describe how to perform the skill.

Step 3. Practice the skill.

---

*Adapted from list of skills included in David W. Johnson and Roger Johnson, *Learning Together and Alone* (Englewood Cliffs, NJ: Prentice-Hall, 1975), p. 97.

Step 4. Receive feedback on performance of the skill.

Step 5. Process learnings about use of the skill.

Step 6. Continue practice until the skill is automatic.

If you follow these six steps, you increase the likelihood that the social skills will become automatic in your students' lives. Students will cooperate not just in groups, but also in the hallway, in other classes, at home, and at church. The payoff for continuing the practice is that the skills are then mastered and used automatically.

Repeat the cycle of six steps to reinforce and to introduce new skills. *All* six steps are important. If groups do not complete a task, or let one person do all the work, or argue about an answer, we suggest that you look at this list. Perhaps you omitted one or more of these crucial steps. You may remedy the problem by repeating the cycle including all the steps in the procedure.

5

The Teacher's Role During Group Work

The stage is now set for your first cooperative group lesson. Your lesson plan is complete, the materials are assembled, and the observation forms are prepared. You have skillfully led students through a discussion and brainstorming of social skills. Your students know that you will be busy observing and recording the use of the social skills that were assigned. They also know that you expect them to depend on themselves and their groupmates to answer questions or solve problems that might arise.

With materials distributed, directions delivered, and hopes high for a successful experience, you watch as students begin to work. You settle yourself near a group, pencil poised above the observation sheet, prepared to observe students so closely that you will not miss a nuance of a social skill. But what is this? The threesome you are observing is arguing over who is going to record. So far no social skills to observe here. You glance up at the sound of angry words and see two students engaged in a shouting match in a nearby group. You suddenly notice hands up in a group across the room. As you consider what to do next, a student approaches and asks, "Can I sharpen my pencil?"

What do you do now? How can you concentrate on your task of observing when there are other distractions and demands? How you deal with these questions and behaviors during this first cooperative group experience is critical. What you do will determine how well students learn to solve their own problems, how often they demand your attention in the future, and whether or not you attempt to do groups again! What you need right now is not a lesson plan, not tips on how to arrange desks, not ideas for building in rewards. What you need is an action plan for dealing with these demands from students. Creating that action plan is the focus for the rest of this chapter.

To begin your plan, you need to decide what type of responses you will make to students. Let's examine two sets of beliefs that affect how you respond. One involves your beliefs about students making mistakes during work time, and the other concerns the teacher's role in solving students' problems.

Teacher Reactions to Student Mistakes

The first step is to define the word "mistake." Webster's definition is "a wrong action or statement proceeding from faulty judgment, inadequate knowledge, or inattention." We like to add the following phrase to this definition: "...that indicates that more practice is needed and more skill lessons are necessary before mastery occurs."

If your belief is that making mistakes shows that students have not yet learned all the necessary skills, you probably look at mistakes as data. When students make mistakes working in groups, you continue to give them chances to practice as well as teach additional lessons on social skills.

If, on the other hand, you believe that mistakes show that students are unwilling or unable to do the task, you are likely to refuse to let students work in groups unless they do it perfectly every time. Since students will not do it perfectly every time because they have not learned the skills, you will probably abandon the use of group work.

Notice that this latter reaction to mistakes made during group work by students is very different from teacher reaction to errors made in subject matter areas. Have you ever heard a teacher say to students, "OK, that's it! No more math for you kids. I'm sick and tired of your mistakes. When you show me that you can do math, then I'll give you some and not until!"? As teachers we realize the need for mistakes in the process of learning any new skill. If students are not making mistakes in math, or spelling, or reading they are not learning anything because they have already learned it. If they never miscalculate, misspell, or misread, we know they have mastered the skill and it is time to move on to a new skill. This means more mistakes and new learning. When it comes to learning social skills there is really no difference in the learning process.

The Teacher's Role in Solving Student Problems

As pointed out in Chapter 2, one of the differences between cooperative groups and typical classroom groups is that teachers use interacting behaviors rather than intervening behaviors when students have problems in groups. This is not because intervening behaviors are wrong and interacting behaviors are right, but because there are very different outcomes for students depending on which types of helping behaviors you tend to use.

If you believe that students need you to solve their problems, chances are that your tendency is to *intervene*. Teachers who use intervening behaviors break into groups (whether they are asked for help or not) to settle arguments, tell students what to do, remind, threaten, give advice, or praise. The belief is that without teacher intervention to motivate and remind, students will not be successful.

If you believe that students are capable of solving their problems independently, you are more likely to *interact* with groups. Teachers who use interacting behaviors interrupt only when asked to help students find solutions. They resist praising students during work time. Instead they give positive feedback during processing (see Chapter 7).

Outcomes for Intervening and Interacting Behaviors

There are short-term and long-term outcomes for both intervening and interacting behaviors. By looking at these outcomes you will be able to decide which type of behavior you want to use consistently when students are working in groups.

Intervening Behaviors

The short-term outcomes for the primary use of intervening behaviors are what most teachers want. Students return to the task, complete the work, and receive the reward. They stop inappropriate behavior or feel good about the praise bestowed upon them by the teacher. The long-term outcomes are less attractive. Students become dependent on the teacher to convince them to keep busy and use social skills. Because it is the teacher's prodding that keeps things rolling, there is little ownership by the group for their success or failure. Since they know that the teacher will bail them out if they have problems, groups do not experience the consequences of not working out their difficulties independently.

Interacting Behaviors

The short-term outcomes for consistently using interacting behaviors are not always pleasant. Without the teacher's intervening, students often spend time, at first, settling arguments and deciding how to work together. As a result, the work is often not completed, so the group does not get the reward. The long-term payoffs, however, are worth the discomfort of using interacting behaviors during your first few cooperative group experiences. When students learn to work things out for themselves, they start to work quickly without relying on the teacher's reminders. They stay on task and ask for help on appropriate occasions. They experience a sense of ownership for their success or failure as a group, and are more likely to put forth the energy to continue to solve problems when they occur. Handling such situations helps students to develop a feeling of power and potency.

Obviously, it is up to you to decide which of these outcomes you desire. If you do not mind students continually looking to you to rescue them or if you require, at all costs, that the assigned work be completed each day, intervention will be your dominant mode. Just be aware of the probable outcomes so that you are not surprised when many hands are in the air and students seem to constantly need your help.

It is important to decide *ahead of time* which behaviors you want to use. Do you prefer to do intervening or interacting behaviors? Do not wait until the questions come, the arguments start, or the loner is ignored. Make that decision now.

Types of Situations Requiring Teacher Input

There are two types of situations which may occur during work time which require a response from you even if that response is to ignore inappropriate behaviors. One type of situation is when students are having difficulty and ask you for help. Their questions sometimes deal with subject matter and sometimes with social skills. If you choose to do intervening behaviors, you will answer every question or respond to every comment made to you. If students ask how to spell a word, you will tell them. If they want to know what the directions are, you will repeat them. If there are complaints about group members, you will listen and solve the problem; this might include behaviors ranging from persuading students to cooperate to breaking up the group.

If you choose to do interacting behaviors, you will ignore some comments and questions, especially when you have told students that you will be doing just that. You might also tell individuals to go back to their group members and check with them. If a group has a question, we suggest that you check to see if this is a question from the whole group or just one person. If it is from the whole group, turn it back to them by asking, "What does your group think?" or "What have you tried so far?" In this way you will discover whether the group needs an academic skill reviewed, such as alphabetical order; or if they need help thinking of ways to solve a social skill problem, such as how to include a groupmate in the group's work.

The other type of situation is when students are obviously having some difficulty and they do not ask you for help. If you choose to do intervening behaviors, you will interrupt the group and tell them what to do, issue threats, give reminders, cajole with praise, or deliver a lecture. This, as we have already explained, will usually take care of the problem immediately, although you might have to return to dispense another dose of intervention later on.

If you choose to use interacting behaviors, you will generally choose to let students deal with the problem(s) themselves. They will either settle the difficulty themselves, ask you for help, or become so disruptive that you may decide to break into the group. We recommend keeping your interruptions to a minimum. Break in only for what you think are serious situations. If you do intervene at this point, use interacting behaviors to return the problem to the group for a solution. You may wish to employ the following procedure:

l) Describe the behavior that you observe.

2) Ask what the group has done so far to solve the problem.

3) Ask what they are going to do next.

4) Brainstorm several solutions with the group if they have no alternatives.

5) Let the group choose a solution to implement.

6) Come back to check on how well the solution is working.

(See Chapter 2 for a description of how interacting problem-solving worked in Mr. Jordan's classroom.)

It may require checking back with the group several times, but turning problems back to the group to solve will result in long-term independent, problem-solving behavior being used by groups.

Test Your Comfort Zone

Whether you do mainly intervening or interacting behaviors, we encourage you to risk moving from the ones you are using now to ones that are more interactive. This does not mean that you ignore every request for help and insist that students solve *all* of their own problems. It does mean that you behave in ways which are more interactive than your usual style. If you generally intervene, decide in what situations you will only interact. Also decide under what circumstances you will intervene. If that occasion does arise, wait a few seconds longer than you normally would, just to stretch yourself and give students a little more time to resolve the problem themselves. Decide on a strategy beforehand so that you will not be as likely to slip back to former behaviors during a classroom crisis.

Action Plan

Now that you have decided which behaviors you want to use, put together an action plan for yourself.

Tell Students

No matter what you decide about your behavior, let students know ahead of time what you will be doing. If you are going to limit the number of questions you will answer to two, inform students of that, as well as how you are going to keep track of how many they have asked. This will save you time and energy later.

Do What You Announce

Do not announce that you will be "invisible" during observation time and then react to students whenever they say anything to you. If you say you are invisible, do not respond to eye contact, talk to students, or interact in any way.

Look for Measures of Success

Decide on one or two small measures of success so that you can maintain motivation for future interacting behaviors. Some measures of success might be that fewer students come up to you when you are observing, or that more of them ignore you when you are observing their groups, or that no one in a group acts differently when you appear. Determine two or three measures which will help you know that your new behaviors are beginning to have an impact.

Process Your New Behaviors

After each cooperative group, notice which of your behaviors you liked and want to continue. Be gentle with yourself. By concentrating on the behavior, rather than bemoaning the things you wish you had done differently, you will make faster progress and enjoy the journey more!

Set Goals for Yourself

After each session, set one specific goal for what you will continue to do or do differently during the next cooperative group lesson. Keep the wording positive. A goal of "I will ignore Paul's name-calling" is more helpful than "I will not get after Paul when he calls his group members names."

We encourage you to examine your beliefs and behaviors in order to develop your action plan. Writing it out is most helpful, but just considering it is also beneficial. You will find it is worth the thought and effort to be prepared for on the spot student demands.

You have decided which of the helping behaviors you plan to use with students and how you are going to put your plan into action. Now it is time to look at some specific ways to help students in terms of how you set up social skills practice, processing sessions, and positive interdependence. Section III of this book will help you to move "beyond beginning."

Section III
Beyond Beginning

6
Social Skills

Does this sound too good to be true? Have you died and gone to teacher heaven if you hear kids say:

"I don't get it, Jane."
"That's okay, Tom. I'll explain it another way."

"Thanks for that idea, Sue. I have never thought of it that way before."

"No, Steve, I don't agree with that answer. Show me how you figured problem 16."

No, you are still alive and well. These are words that can be heard from students in cooperative groups. Although you probably did not hear such skilled responses in your first group lesson, they do occur, but not by accident.

Over and over again, teachers have asked students to work on an assignment in groups, with added directions of "Get along," or "Cooperate." You have said that to students; we have, too. But, we all know that such statements are not sufficient. Students need to learn the skills of cooperation right from scratch, just as they need to learn math facts and basal words. We need to teach them those cooperative skills, step by step. In this chapter, we will:

- Look at what social skills are and why they are necessary

- Consider which skills to use when beginning cooperative groups and how to progress in the use of social skills

- Outline the steps that are necessary to teach social skills as well as the procedure for observing how often students use them

- Take a glimpse at how to phase out the assignment of social skills

Rethinking Leadership

Leadership looks and sounds different in cooperative groups than in typical classroom groups. It will be helpful if you and your students examine old definitions of leadership and establish new pictures from which to work.

Student leaders abound in schools. Some class leaders exhibit positive characteristics when they:

- Volunteer for duties

- Initiate pro-social activities

- Maintain positive attitudes towards teachers, peers, and school

- Enter fully into school life

These leaders are often the academic achievers, the class officers, and the athletes who are team members.

Other student leaders exhibit negative characteristics when they:

- Exhibit isolation, alone or in an antisocial gang

- Decline or ignore positive activities

- Initiate misbehavior

- Scorn everyday school life

These are the leaders that educators often try to ignore, hope will outgrow their behavior, or pass on to the next grade.

In classrooms, teachers often use the positive leader to advance academic goals by selecting them to oversee class activities, especially in group work. One of two things is likely to happen:

- The chosen leader succeeds in organizing the group into some semblance of a productive unit

- The chosen leader ends up doing all the work for the group, resenting being put-upon and is disliked by the group for being productive

The negative leaders are often ignored, dispersed among groups with the hope that they will not spoil projects, or corralled into a group where they sabotage only themselves. Their influence is seen as an irritation to normal classroom procedures.

Neither type of leader was born with those characteristics, nor were they handed their behaviors along with the roles they have learned to play. Both positive and negative student leaders learn to repeat and refine their behaviors, consciously or subconsciously, as they receive the rewards of attention and reinforcement from adults and their peers. Since both sorts of leaders have power with their peers, this power of leadership may be channeled by teachers to positive advantage.

Leadership in cooperative groups involves the use of social skills by *all* group members. By practicing social skills:

- Positive leaders learn to share their behaviors and rewards

- Negative leaders learn to channel their behaviors into useful activities while still receiving attention from peers and adults

- Followers learn the skills of positive leadership thereby receiving both extrinsic and intrinsic rewards

Every member can win in cooperative groups. We will now look at the skills required to make everyone a leader.

Social Skills: The Definition Reviewed

First we will review the definition and types of social skills. Social skills are those specific behaviors performed by all group members which help the group complete the task and like each other when the task is finished. David Johnson and Roger Johnson have categorized social skills as either ''task'' skills or ''maintenance'' skills. Both types must be practiced consistently if the group is to maintain itself as a positive, effective unit.

Task Skills

In the process of completing a specific task, there are many discrete behaviors involved. Task skills have a content focus and are necessary whether the job is to make a list, draw a picture, memorize facts, complete a project, or answer a sheet of questions.

You are already familiar with ''Share information and ideas'' and ''Check for understanding.'' Other examples of task social skills are:

- Giving ideas

- Keeping track of time

- Following directions

If none of the group members perform task skills, the group founders and fails to meet its subject matter objective. The consistent use of these skills helps the group work effectively to create a high-quality product.

Maintenance Skills

In order for the group to continue working effectively together, it is not sufficient to complete the task. There must also be an emphasis on each individual group member. Such emphasis builds group cohesiveness and stability.

We have already introduced the skills ''Check for agreement'' and ''Encourage others.'' Other maintenance skills are:

- Addressing group members by name

- Sharing feelings

- Responding to ideas

Use of these skills helps students feel better about themselves, each other and the group. Without these behaviors, a group single-mindedly completes the task with little acknowledgement of the individuals involved. Without such caring, groups rarely enjoy the process or want to continue meeting on a regular basis.

Both task and maintenance skills are necessary for groups to work effectively. If a group completes the task, but none of the members ever wants to see or work with the others again, that is not a successful cooperative group. If, on the other hand, a group has a wonderful time and everyone feels cared for and respected but the task was not finished, that is not a successful cooperative group either. The goal of teaching social skills is the creation of groups which consist of positive, on-task students who enjoy their time together, care about each other, and produce high quality work.

There are many social skills that you may introduce to your students. We have suggestions to assist you when choosing beginning skills as well as a list of skills from which to choose for future cooperative group experiences.

Beginning Social Skills

The first social skills chosen for cooperative groups must do two things:

- Motivate students to do the assigned work

- Motivate students to work together

In light of these considerations, it was recommended in Chapter 3 that you choose from four fundamental social skills:

- **Task Skills**

  Check for understanding

  Share information and ideas

- **Maintenance Skills**

  Encourage

  Check for agreement

These skills provide the initial task and maintenance motivation required to get a cooperative group started. No matter which ones you began with in your first lesson plan, add the additional two or three before you go on to others. They will provide a foundation of social skills upon which your groups will be able to build cooperation.

There are also more advanced skills you may introduce to your students. A list of typical social skills that successful group members use follows:

Additional Social Skills

Task Skills

Lower Elementary	Upper El/Jr. High	Senior High/Adult
Check others' understanding of the work	Check others' understanding of the work	Check others' understanding of the work
Give ideas	Contribute ideas	Give information & opinions
Talk about work	Stay on-task	Stay on-task
Get group back to work	Get group back to work	Get group back to work
Repeat what has been said	Paraphrase	Paraphrase
Ask questions	Ask questions	Seek information & opinions
Follow directions	Follow directions	Follow directions
Stay in seat	Stay in own space	

Maintenance Skills

Lower Elementary	Upper El/Jr. High	Senior High/Adult
Encourage	Encourage	Encourage
Use names	Use names	Use names
Invite others to talk	Encourage others to talk	Encourage others to talk
Respond to ideas	Respond to ideas	Acknowledge contributions
Look at others	Use eye contact	Use eye contact
Say "Thank you"	Show appreciation	Express appreciation
Share feelings	Share feelings	Share feelings
Disagree in a nice way	Disagree in an agreeable way	Disagree in an agreeable way
Keep things calm	Keep things calm	Reduce tension
		Practice Active Listening

As you can see from the three columns, the skills necessary to work in groups are the same from preschool through graduate school. It is only the vocabulary that changes. Choose the words that best fit your students regardless of the columns to which you refer. For example, some junior high students prefer to call encouraging behaviors "cheerleading" since that is a role with which they are familiar.

Although this list may look complete, it is not. Please notice the blank after each column. This indicates that there are many more social skills than the ones listed here. Social skills arise from need—what the group perceives it needs to operate more effectively as well as what the teacher perceives the group needs. If a group is having trouble because group members are not in their seats, it is time to have "Stay in seat" as a social skill. If some group members are having trouble sharing the calculator or the clay, "Share materials" becomes a necessary social skill to practice. If students use insults consistently, then a necessary social skill is "Talk positively to one another."

However, at this point, we would like to offer a gentle reminder. While you want your students to use all of these and other social skills as well, it is not reasonable to expect mastery of all of them in any given school year. We suggest that you pick several skills that are important to you in your particular classroom setting. Introduce those to your students, based on their proficiency in the area of cooperation.

Introducing and teaching social skills are not your only jobs as a cooperative group facilitator. In the beginning it is also necessary that you observe groups practicing social skills. We will now look at how you do that.

Observation of Social Skills

There are three ways to observe groups using social skills. You may do an objective observation, an anecdotal observation, or an informal observation. All of these methods provide data for groups. In this section, we examine the three methods and uses of the data, as well as ways to organize and use this valuable information. (See Chapter 7 for how to share this information with students.)

Objective Observation

The teacher does objective observations of students working in groups to provide them with data about the frequency of social skill use. The teacher moves from group to group making a tally mark each time a social skill being used is observed. (See Chapter 4, for a complete explanation of how to observe and what types of forms to use.) Not only do students benefit from actual data about the frequency of appropriate behavior, but they also get the message that these behaviors are so important that the teacher will look and listen for them during work time. By observing their use of social skills during work time, the teacher demonstrates that in this classroom students and the teacher do more than talk about social skills—they use them!

We find that there are three occasions when doing objective observations is especially helpful. Such objective observations prove helpful because the teacher wants students to be conscious of how often they are using social skills. The three occasions include:

- When first starting cooperative learning

- When new social skills are introduced

- When student behavior in groups become disruptive and unproductive

Anecdotal Observation

Anecdotal observations involve the teacher completing an observation form recording the actual words heard and the behaviors seen instead of making a tally mark each time social skills are used.

The purpose of anecdotal feedback is to:

- Help students realize the importance of their behaviors

- Give students information on what their behaviors look like and sound like during group work

- Make students aware of behaviors that are performed unconsciously so that decisions can be made about which behaviors to continue and which to eliminate

Use anecdotal feedback:

- After students have processed several cooperative groups

- After students have experienced several objective observations and feedback

- When students become conscious of practicing social skills

- When no specific social skills are assigned

We have developed two forms to be used during anecdotal observations. The first is used when social skills have been assigned. This sample form has been completed to give you an idea of behaviors to notice during work time.

Anecdotal Observation Form—Assigned Skills				
SKILLS: Share ideas			**Respond to ideas**	
Names	Verbal	Non-Verbal	Verbal	Non-Verbal
Jill	*I think...* *What do you think about this...*			*Nod, smile*
Mary		*Wrote suggested word on paper*	*Yes, and...* *Yes, but...*	*Raised eye brows* *Shrugged*
Jack	*I say that we...*		*Are you saying that...What do you mean?*	*Laughed*

As you move from group to group, write down the exact words you hear and the specific behaviors you see that are relative to the prescribed social skills. Remain long enough or return later in order to record something positive for every group member. This helps even the most reluctant group member to feel that he or she is a contributing groupmate.

The second form is used when no social skills have been assigned. Move from group to group, writing down specific words and behaviors that appear to help or hinder the group's completion of the task or getting along together. Be sure to include verbal comments as well as non-verbal behaviors. (See Appendix D for a sample copy of these forms.)

	Anecdotal Observation Form—Without Assigned Skills			
	Helpful Behaviors		**Unhelpful Behaviors**	
Names	**Verbal**	**Non-Verbal**	**Verbal**	**Non-Verbal**
Ken	*Thanks for that idea*	*Smile*	*Shut-up*	*Pinch*
Phil	*So you think we should...*	*Nod*		*Grabbed pencil*
Janey	*Let's get moving. We have 5 minutes left*	*Looked at clock*	*Take your hands off the paper*	

Informal Observation

An informal observation may be used by the teacher when social skills are not assigned. You may ask students to notice the social skills they use, or tell students that you will be the only person collecting data.

Feedback from the informal observation may be useful to:

- Reinforce students for the skills they do practice

- Provide information for teachers about whether or not certain skills have been mastered

- Provide information for teachers to help them determine whether or not to phase out certain skills

For an informal observation form, you can use a piece of notebook paper divided into two columns. Label the left column ''Social Skills'' and label the right column ''Behaviors'' (see a sample copy of this form in Appendix D). Move from group to group. On the left side of the paper, jot down the social skill you notice (for example, ''Keep track of time''). Then on the right side, write specific uses of the skills, such as: ''Looking at clock,'' and spoken phrases such as ''Let's get going,'' or ''We'd better move to the next problem.'' For this observation, it is not necessary to record who used each skill.

Organization and Use of Observation Data

You and the students go to a lot of trouble to collect and examine observation data. It would be a shame to just throw it away. We have two suggestions for keeping track of that valuable information.

Class List. You have started a "Looks Like/Sounds Like" list for social skills. Record any helpful behaviors you noticed during your observations which are not already listed on chart paper. You may have heard some new encouraging words, for example, or seen some different ways to check for understanding. Record these while students are processing or as you mention them during your feedback. Also record student suggestions. If these specific words and actions are reviewed before the next cooperative lesson, they serve as a reminder of appropriate behavior.

Group Folders. If groups are staying together for several activities, a group folder helps keep all written information organized. The folder may contain goals for social skills, unfinished work, corrected work, as well as observation forms. These observation forms are useful as evidence of growth in social skills as well as an indication of areas needing improvement.

Social Skills: The Goal

Task skills. Maintenance skills. Will you *always* have to teach, assign, and observe social skills when using cooperative groups? The answer is "No!" Those three procedures are initial techniques to insure that students understand and practice the skills of cooperation. The ultimate goal is that students will cooperate, whether or not they are assigned skills or working in a cooperative group.

Eventually you will not have to attend to social skills. But how will you know when it is time to phase them out?

These are some behaviors that you might notice:

• You see nods, smiles, students leaning into the work.

• You hear kind words; disagreeing in an agreeable way; a phrase like, "We are off task, let's get back to work," and a groupmate answers, "Thanks, Tom, for reminding us."

• You notice the isolated student joining in class life and liking it; the "boss" asking for someone else's opinion; papers being handed in on time because everyone helped.

When you reach this point, you will have to employ targeted use of social skill review and procedures only when a situation calls for brand new skills or problems with individuals, groups, or the class indicate a need.

Having reached the ultimate goal, you will be ready to say, "Here is your cooperative group assignment. GO!"

7
Social Skills Processing

Assigning social skills for students to practice will result in the improvement of your classroom groups. You will notice students talking to one another more, using more encouraging words, and sharing materials more often. If, however, you want to obtain maximum results for your efforts, we recommend that you include the strategy of processing after every cooperative group lesson.

Processing is a procedure by which students examine how they practiced social skills, how they could use them more effectively next time, as well as where else in their lives these skills might be helpful. Processing on a consistent basis increases the use of positive group behaviors and also decreases the number of times social skills must be practiced before they become integrated into your students' group behavior patterns.

Without processing, cooperative groups are often only groups of students sitting together working on the same task, rather than groups of students learning how to cooperate. Most classroom teachers trained in cooperative learning realize that there is only limited improvement on social skills without processing.

A ninth grade drafting teacher told us that he could not understand why his students continued to use many unfriendly behaviors during group work. He was especially puzzled because he had built in social skills and positive interdependence, but he had not seen the consistent improvement in student behaviors he had expected. The problem was revealed by his response to our question, "How do they deal with these unhelpful behaviors and the negative feelings they produce during processing?" His answer was, "Oh, we rarely have time for processing." After a brief review he realized that what was seemingly a negative group experience could have been a source of learning. This teacher began to schedule time for processing in order to give his students the opportunity to learn from their group experiences.

In this chapter, we will discuss how to set up processing experiences so that students analyze and evaluate their social skill behavior. From these learnings they can set goals or apply new understandings to other group situations. Your role is to encourage students to commit themselves to their own opinions regarding their behavior and to process the group experiences that they have lived. Later in the chapter we describe how you can share your observations and opinions in ways that allow your students to trust their own perceptions while using your input to help them improve their skills. Processing time then becomes an opportunity for you to help your students grow toward independent thinking and problem-solving.

In this chapter we also discuss specific steps and methods to help you and your students have a successful experience with processing. Although careful pre-planning may prevent common problems from occurring, sometimes preventive measures are not effective. For that reason, in the last section of this chapter, we describe problems that may occur during processing. A range of possibilities for you to consider in finding your own solutions is also provided.

Processing Methods

There are many methods for conducting processing with students of all ages. We offer several which the K-12 teachers with whom we work have found most effective. Feel free to create your own methods after you are familiar with these.

Processing begins as soon as the subject matter has been completed or work time is over. Even if the work will be continued in the next session, each day's use of social skills is processed immediately. Allow 5 to 15 minutes before the end of the allotted cooperative group time for processing. Some teachers write the time on the board or set a timer so that everyone knows when it is time to stop, check papers, hand in work, or clean up in preparation for processing.

The teacher gives students several statements regarding social skill behaviors. Students react to these by either filling in the blanks or responding to statements.

Fill in the Blank/Finish the Sentence

Students respond with a word or phrase to fill in the blank or finish the sentence.

Example: ''A social skill we enjoyed practicing today was _____ because _____

_____ .''

Responding to Statements

Students respond to statements based on their own opinions. Each of the following sample statements can be used when you have students respond by Forced Choice, Values Voting, or Continuums. (See Appendix E for additional statements.)

Sample Statements:

''Others in the group helped me when I had a question.''

''We disagreed in a nice way.''

''I used names when talking to my groupmates.''

Forced Choice—Students make a choice between a set of two or three responses. The teacher reads each statement (see samples above) from the board or a duplicated copy. Students respond by marking one choice, responding orally, or choosing non-verbally. We observed a group of kindergarten students draw a happy face on one side of a paper plate, and a sad face on the opposite side. They then used these ''signs'' to indicate their responses to the statements.

Sample sets of responses:

Never/Sometimes/Always

No/Yes

A Little/Some/A Lot

Values Voting—The teacher tells students the response choices for voting. (Writing or drawing them on the board is helpful.) Each statement (see samples above) is read aloud. Silent thinking time is given. Then everyone votes at the same time when the teacher says "Vote." This procedure helps prevent students voting the way their friends do and encourages them to express their own opinions.

Choices for Responses:

Younger Students

Yes—Thumb up

No—Thumb down

Agree—Hand in air

No comment
Don't know } —Arms folded

Disagree—Thumb down

Older Students

Strongly agree—Wave hand in air

Agree—Hand in air

No comment
Don't know } —Arms folded

Disagree—Thumb down

Strongly disagree—Wave thumb down

Continuums—Students put an "X" somewhere on the line between "Always" and "Never." This indicates where they feel they were on the social skills assigned for that day's lesson.

ALWAYS   NEVER

Continuums can be done on paper or by making a human continuum along a wall or line on the classroom floor. Both ends of the line are identified and students place themselves on the line where they feel their "X" belongs.

Teacher's Role During Student Response Time

In order for students to feel safe in risking their opinions, an atmosphere of trust and acceptance must be established. You can create this atmosphere in your classroom by discussing and enforcing the following guidelines whenever students are invited to publicly respond in class. These guidelines for teachers and students apply whether the reaction is an oral response, a vote, or choosing a spot on the continuum.

- All answers are correct.

- All positions are respected, whether agreed with or not.

- No group members may force anyone else to agree with their answer.

- There are no negative comments about one's self or others.

It is as important to follow these guidelines yourself as it is to make sure your students follow them. It is important for you to withhold your judgment of student responses, whether you agree or disagree. Students will be watching you closely. If you say "Good!" to some responses, and say nothing about or frown at others, students will quickly learn that all answers are *not* correct.

For example, if a group of students votes that they stayed on task and you know that they barely started on the assigned work, accept their opinion with no comment. Later you will have an opportunity to share your observations and opinions. At this time you may have them confront the discrepancy. Give students the space to risk their own points of view even though it may sometimes be uncomfortable for you.

How To Select Processing Statements

The selection of statements for use during processing depends upon several factors, including the reading skill level of students, time available and the teacher's desire for a varied approach. Less skilled readers may respond non-verbally or orally. Skilled readers are more able to offer written responses. Even though your students are capable of responding in writing, do not hesitate to have them use Values Voting, for example, when time is limited or a change of pace is in order.

Two other considerations which impact the selection of processing statements are the focus and type.

Selecting by Focus

You will choose the point of focus when students are processing. Do they focus on self, others, or the group as a whole? In the first few cooperative group lessons, we suggest that you have students focus on the group as a whole. Use statements that deal with "we," "us," and "our group." This focus is recommended since it is easier to analyze "us" than "me" or "you." (See Chapter 3 for details about beginning processing statements and procedure.) After students have experienced cooperative groups and processing sessions several times, ask them to focus on themselves ("what I did") or on each other ("what you did") as well as on the group as a whole.

Selecting by Type

There are three types of processing from which to choose. They are Analysis, Application, and Goal Setting.

Analysis means that all responses deal with the group experience just completed. It is an attempt to help students discover what was a help and what was a hindrance in completing the day's group work. Students analyze whether specific behaviors had a positive or negative effect on group progress or morale. In Analysis Processing, the focus is on *I*, *you*, or *we*.

Focusing on *I* helps each student individually consider how she or he performed in the group. This is especially beneficial for students who tend to disown responsibility for negative group outcomes by blaming others.

Examples: "I followed directions."

"A social skill I enjoyed practicing today was _____ because

_____ ."

Using *you* as a focus gives students a chance to give someone else in the group feedback about which of his or her behaviors were perceived as helpful or unhelpful. This is an especially effective focus for processing at ages when peer pressure and influence are strong. Student feedback can often be more motivating than teacher feedback.

Examples: "Others looked at me when I was talking."

"I really felt good when others in my group _____

_____ ."

Focusing on *we* forces the group to reach consensus on one response. The goal is to get input from every member and reach agreement.

Examples: "The social skill we used the least was _____ because

_____ ."

"Today we took turns in our group."

Application deals with what students learned from this group experience that could be applied to other situations. Often teachers erroneously assume that students understand the connections between what happens in the classroom and what happens in the rest of their world. Using social skills in cooperative groups does not guarantee their use in other classroom activities, in the hallway, on the playground, or in the cafeteria. By including processing in cooperative groups, we provide opportunities for students to make connections between classroom cooperation and cooperative experiences in the rest of their lives. It helps them examine group interactions at school, home, church, and in the community. Only by understanding the value of cooperation will students apply these lessons to other places besides the second-hour math class or the Tuesday reading lesson.

In Application Processing, the focus is on individuals responding to an "I" statement, then sharing with the group, or the group working together on a "we" statement.

Examples: "One thing I learned about group work is _____

_____ ."

"We learned that in any group it is helpful to _____

_____ ."

Goal setting gives students an opportunity to choose a specific social skill to use more effectively at the next cooperative group lesson. This is either a skill that they have not mastered or one they have practiced before but did not use in today's lesson.

In Goal Setting Processing the focus can be on goals for individual group members or a goal for the group as a whole.

Examples: "One social skill I will practice more consistently next time is _____

_____ ."

"I will do this by _____ ,

_____ , and _____ ."
(three specific behaviors)

"Our group will encourage each other next time we meet by _____

_____ ."

(specific behavior)

We recommend that you choose at least one type of processing and preferably two. If you choose only one, use *Analysis Processing*. Analysis Processing gives students a chance to analyze a particular group experience . Such an analysis paves the way for more positive behaviors and outcomes in subsequent group work.

If you choose two types of processing, there is a "rule of thumb" for choosing between Application or Goal Setting Processing. If group members will be in different groups for the next lesson, use Application Processing. If they will be in the same group, use Goal Setting Processing since this type is most appropriate when students have an opportunity to actually work toward the goals they set.

If you choose all three types of processing, be prepared for more than 15 minutes of processing time. Adequate coverage of the three types is time-consuming. (See Appendix E for additional examples of processing statements.)

Procedure for Processing

If you were deciding on processing for tomorrow's cooperative groups by reading this chapter, you would have made the following decisions by now:

- **Processing methods to use**

  Fill in the Blank/Finish the Sentence

  or

  Responding to Statements

- **Processing statements to use**

  Focus—I, you, we

  and

  Type—Analysis, Application, Goal Setting

A sequence for processing that many teachers find beneficial follows. (Notice the choices you have in Steps #5 and #6.)

1. Decide beforehand what specific processing statements to use.

2. Write the statements on the board or distribute duplicated copies. (Even if you teach young children, writing processing statements on the board is a reminder for you and any helpers in the room.)

3. Read aloud the processing statements as a way to let students know what to expect after work time.

4. After group work is done, review the processing statements and procedure.

5. (Choose 1)

☐ Students share their reactions orally in their group, or write them and then share with one another.

☐ Students discuss individual opinions and reach consensus on a ''we'' statement.

6. (Choose 1)

☐ A spokesperson reports ''we'' statements to the whole class. The other students listen as the teacher records the reactions on chart paper.

☐ The teacher goes around to groups as they finish and hears individual responses or the group's response from the spokesperson.

7. The teacher gives feedback to students based upon observations of group behavior on social skills. (See next section of this chapter.)

8. Processing sheets and written teacher observations are filed in a folder for each group. Before the next session of cooperative group work, students refer to these processing sheets or the teacher reviews the reactions recorded on chart paper. This helps students to focus on appropriate social skill behavior before they begin group work. (See Appendix F for sample processing sheets.)

We have described how to set up processing sessions so that your students may learn from their experiences. As we have done this, we have admonished you several times to hold onto your opinions until your students have had an opportunity to express themselves. Now it is your turn! Information follows about how to present your opinions and feedback so that your students feel respected, encouraged, and motivated to apply their learnings.

Teacher Feedback During Processing

Students are so used to hearing teacher opinions, judgments, praise, criticism, suggestions, directions, and advice, that it is easy for them to develop the habit of not thinking for themselves. They may find that not only is it easier to wait for the teacher's opinion; but usually the teacher's opinion is the only one that counts! Rarely do students have the opportunity to give their opinions about their own work; even more rarely are those opinions solicited by the teacher. Small wonder that when students are asked for their opinions about their behaviors during processing, they are usually either reluctant or unskilled at giving them.

We recommend that you give your feedback after students give theirs. If you go first with your observations, students may copy what you have noticed and attempt to produce the ''right'' answer. If you go first with your opinions about helpful and unhelpful behaviors, students have no need to analyze themselves and the success of their groups. If you want to help students think for themselves, processing time is an important opportunity. We hear teachers everywhere ask, ''Why won't my students think for themselves? They're always asking me if something is long enough, short enough, red enough, blue enough, neat enough. Enough! Why can't they trust their own opinions?'' The reason is that we teachers have taught them to turn to us for evaluation of their work. As a result, they have not learned to form their own opinions and trust their own perceptions.

You can help students learn how to be more confident of themselves and their opinions by changing the ways you react. The ways that teachers praise and criticize have a profound effect on students' self-images, confidence, and achievement.* Be conscious of your words and behaviors, and use some different ways to share your opinions. You can more effectively motivate students to reach their potential and trust themselves by using such methods.

We have found that in order for teacher input to be the most beneficial to students' growth it needs to be:

- Planned

- Specific

- Consistent

- Brief

- Timely

If teacher input is haphazard and non-specific, students often do not pay attention. They are likely to "tune out" the teacher's voice. To encourage students to "tune in," consider the following methods of giving your feedback and opinions on student behavior. Then decide how you can best give students information which they can use to congratulate themselves for the work just completed as well as to improve future efforts.

Giving Feedback

As we discussed in Chapter 6, there are three types of observations that teachers can choose to make—objective, anecdotal and informal. All of them will help you gather information to share with your students about their performance on social skills during group work time.

After you have observed and your students have done their processing, it is time for you to share the information collected. We recommend the 7-step procedure which follows for giving this feedback to students.

Step 1. Give the observation form information to each group.

Step 2. Allow time for students to compare your information with their conclusions.

Step 3. Check with groups whose opinions conflict with your observations.

Step 4. Share with the class appropriate behaviors which you have observed.

Step 5. Describe to students the unhelpful behaviors you noticed during work time.

Step 6. See that all the groups' papers are filed.

Step 7. Do teacher processing of the lesson.

---

*Arthur L. Costa, *The Enabling Behaviors* (San Anselmo, CA: Search Models Unlimited, 1983), p. 58.

Explanation of Steps

Step 1. Give the observation form information to each group. To do this, hand each group its observation form or give the information to each person in the small group. Look at students, using their names and speaking directly to them. For example, "Marie, I observed you checking seven times and encouraging three times." For anecdotal observations you might say, "Lewis, your helpful behaviors were taking turns with the scissors and asking a question about how to spell a word. Your unhelpful behavior was calling Jim a name."

Do not compare students to one another or to other groups. This leads to feelings of competition and separateness which are not desirable in creating a cooperative classroom environment.

Step 2. Allow time for students to compare your information with their conclusions. Give two or three minutes for students to discuss the comparisons between the information on the observation form and their completed processing statements. How does the teacher feedback agree with or differ from the group's responses? How can any discrepancy be explained?

For example, if encouraging is observed only one time and yet group members all state that they felt encouraged, there may be a discrepancy. If the group puts an "X" on "Always" on the group continuum and the teacher observed encouraging words and actions 40 times, there is no discrepancy. If the teacher has observed only unhelpful behaviors and the group thinks they were successful, there is a discrepancy.

Step 3. Check with groups whose opinions conflict with your observations. Go to each of the groups where you noticed a discrepancy and determine whether or not they have noted this. If not, point it out. If they have, move to the next group.

Step 4. Share with the class appropriate behaviors which you have observed. Bring the whole class together and share any new ways you have observed social skills being used in a helpful way. Collect and record any use of skills that students noticed on the lists of appropriate social skill behaviors which have already been started.

Step 4 sounds simple. What is so difficult about telling students about the behaviors they exhibited which helped the group? The problem is that teachers often turn these comments into praise. We are not opposed to praise. What does concern us is that the two types of praise create very different outcomes. One type is called *evaluative* praise and the other is called *descriptive* praise.*

Evaluative praise sounds like:

"Your group did a really good job today."

Descriptive praise sounds like:

"I heard people saying 'Please' and 'Thank you' in your group today. I saw materials being shared by everyone. These behaviors helped your group work well together."

Evaluative praise shows teacher approval but gives no specifics in terms of appropriate behavior. Descriptive praise describes these behaviors as well as their effect.

---

*Haim Ginott, *Between Teacher and Child* (New York, NY: The MacMillan Co., 1972), p. 125.

Using evaluative praise creates a short-term benefit because students are often motivated by it. Words like "excellent," "great," "fantastic," "wonderful," all give students immediate teacher approval. The problem is that long-term evaluative praise creates dependency on the teacher. Students must continually check with you to make sure that they receive your approval.

Descriptive praise can be equally as motivational once students get used to it. It requires some practice for students to acquire the knack of hearing your descriptive words and then saying to themselves, "I did a good job," or "We really were great at cooperating today." This sort of self-praise results in a long-term benefit because students become their own sources of approval. They no longer feel constantly compelled to look only to the teacher for measures of their success.

Evaluative praise can also create feelings of competition and hostility within a classroom because of labeling, judging, and comparing.

> "Group 2 is the best today because they finished first. Great job!"

> "Sarah did more encouraging than anyone else today. She's terrific!"

Those who do not receive praise may work harder to earn it the next time. However, in such cases, students are still dependent on the teacher's approval. This does not help them trust their own opinions. Even labeling the entire class as "good" is not as helpful as telling them specifically about observed behaviors which were friendly, polite, appropriate, or helpful.

When you give descriptive praise to students in the privacy of their small groups, look at the individual, use his or her name, and tell how this individual's behavior in the group contributed to the outcomes for the group.

> "Jim, your encouraging Pete seemed to help him keep working. When you said, "You can do it!" he smiled, sat up straight, took a breath, and continued with his spelling work."

If you praise the class, do it descriptively rather than evaluatively.

> "I noticed that your groups worked effectively today. People expressed their ideas and when someone didn't, he or she was asked for his or her opinion. That helped everyone stay involved."

The examples below further illustrate the difference between evaluative and descriptive praise. Notice which type of praise would be more useful to students in recognizing the positive behaviors which you would like to see continued.

Evaluative Praise	**Descriptive Praise**
"Good work on social skills."	"I saw smiles and eye contact. Everyone cheered when the work was finished. Your group acted like a team."
"Excellent work in your group today."	"You shared materials in your group. People took turns. I heard soft voices. Your group helped our classroom stay relaxed and calm."

"I'm proud of your group."

"Group members disagreed with one another in friendly ways. People used paraphrasing, nodding, and parroting to show group members they were heard. I understand how your group gets along so well."

Step 5. Describe to students the unhelpful behaviors you noticed during work time. Just as it is important to praise descriptively, it is important to criticize descriptively. Descriptive criticism gives students information about behaviors that are disruptive to the group:

"When you wouldn't take your turn to read, Madeline, you did not contribute your share to the group. That was not helpful behavior."

Evaluative criticism labels students and can create resentment and resistance:

"You were uncooperative, Madeline. I'm shocked at your behavior."

Using negative comments and labels when criticizing students only helps them learn how to criticize their peers by using negative comments and labels. We can model helpful ways to criticize in cooperative groups by doing so ourselves during the processing session.

Criticism that encourages students to change their behavior has the following characteristics:*

- *Focuses on the behavior rather than on the person.* "You're rude" focuses on Bill as a person. "You interrupted Mary three times when she started to give her opinion," focuses on Bill's behavior.

- *Involves sharing information rather than giving advice or threatening.* "I don't like people being called Stupid or Dummy. I expect you to settle your differences by discussion, not name-calling." This descriptive criticism leaves students the space to decide what to do with the information and how to improve. "You'd better knock off the name-calling or you'll stay after school," allows little room for students to decide what to do or how to do it.

- *Involves only one or two behaviors.* There may be many behaviors that you do not want students to continue. However, if you mention all of them, you reduce the possibility that students will be able to do *any* of them. Choose only one or two of the most crucial behaviors. Ignore the others for now.

- *Is avoided when you or the other person have strong feelings such as anger, frustration, or impatience.* It is more helpful to give criticism when everyone is calm. If emotions are running high, talk with the person or group later, or give your feedback the next day before the group work begins.

---

*Adapted from list included in Jean Illsley Clark's newsletter, *WE: Newsletter for Nurturing Support Groups* (16535 9th Ave. N., Plymouth, MN 55447), V. 4, #3, January-February, 1983, pg. 5.

Notice in the examples below the differences between descriptive and evaluative criticism.

Evaluative Criticism	**Descriptive Criticism**
"You did a poor job today."	"I noticed people grabbing materials from one another. I saw frowns and heard angry words. That's not using social skills."
"Don't ever let me catch you doing that again."	"People who hit others will have to work alone."
"You're a bunch of spoiled brats."	"I saw people writing on each other's papers without permission. That's why some group members were angry."

If you give criticism to the class, mention behaviors only, not names. When you are sharing criticism in a small group, look at the person, say the person's name, and address the criticism to that individual. Resist labeling the group. ("You were all really mean to each other.") If you feel that criticism is in order, do it descriptively and without mentioning names. ("People are not for hitting. Name calling and angry words do not settle arguments.")

When sharing both praise and criticism during processing sessions, these four guidelines are important:

- Describe the behavior clearly.

- Do not evaluate the person doing the behavior.

- State the effect the behavior has on the situation.

- Do not compare people or groups.

Remember, the purpose of processing is to give students an opportunity to use their own intelligence and perception. It is not a time for the teacher to get on a bandwagon or a soapbox.

Step 6. See that all the groups' papers are filed. Make sure observation forms, unfinished work, and processing sheets are placed in each group's folder. At first, to be sure that everything is included, check these folders yourself. Later, each group makes sure that everything is included, then turns in the folder to the teacher or files it in the appropriate place.

Step 7. Do your processing of the lesson. Just as students learn from processing their experiences, so do teachers. Immediately after, or the same day, take five minutes to analyze the lesson. Determine what worked and what did not. Analyze your behavior and set goals for yourself. What type of observation would be most useful for you to do the next time? What method of processing would be appropriate? How can you intervene less and interact more? How can you be more descriptive and less evaluative? By taking a few minutes to process your cooperative group experiences, you will have learned from what happened instead of wishing that group experiences had been "better."

Your processing of the lesson may also include decisions about which social skills to assign for the next cooperative group session. If students have done Goal Setting Processing, then they will already have one social skill on which to work. We recommend that you choose additional social skills for groups based on student processing results, observation data, and your own perceptions.

For example, when a group has difficulty being specific about which behaviors they used when practicing "Respond to ideas," it could be that they did not practice that skill. The observation data you collected may indicate that you observed your students responding to ideas only once during the time you were there. Using your perceptions and observations, you may remember that one person filled out the answer sheet, only rarely consulting the other two groupmates. Based on all of this information, your conclusion could be to assign the social skill of "Share ideas and information" or "Check for agreement." These skills would encourage students to include everyone in the group process.

As you continue to repeat this decision-making after each cooperative group lesson, notice, too, whether a group uses more maintenance or more task social skills. If group members continually have trouble getting along with one another, assign maintenance skills. If they often do not complete the work, put more emphasis on task skills. Use all of your resources as you continue to assess needs and assign social skills.

Roadblocks To Processing

road·block (rōd' blăk)—n. an element from outside or inside oneself that causes temporary difficulties in reaching a goal. *syn.* see obstacle, hurdle, challenge.

Even though you have followed all of our suggestions and instructions for setting up and conducting processing, you may find that problems have surfaced (as they do every day in the classroom). As you can see from the above definition of *roadblock* (taken from the Dishon and Wilson O'Leary Unabridged Dictionary), we view these problems as only temporary setbacks. Even the best efforts to prevent roadblocks from occurring will not work 100% of the time. We encourage you to see sources of problems not as evidence of failure, but as a challenge and a learning opportunity.

In this section we share the most common roadblocks that teachers run into when setting up and conducting processing sessions. Several possible remedies which have worked for other teachers are listed here. Look them over carefully to see if there are answers or suggestions that may be helpful for you. If not, use the list as a stepping stone toward finding your own answers.

Roadblock: Not Enough Time For Processing

There are numerous reasons for this problem. Fire drills, announcements, buses arriving late or departing early, unannounced assemblies, direction-giving that takes longer than planned—all of these situations influence your carefully planned and protected time for processing.

Possible Remedies:

- Do quick processing (Values Voting or Forced Choice).

- Finish work next time. Do processing now.

- Send work home as homework. Do processing now.

- Do processing next time.

Roadblock: Superficial Processing

This roadblock is evident when responses to processing are vague, when some students or groups are not involved in processing, or when processing is not completed.

Answers Are Vague. This occurs when you get the same answer repeated over and over; "Yes" or "No" answers with no explanation; or responses like "We cooperated," "We did OK," or "We did a good job."

Possible Remedies:

- Use the processing statements suggested in this guidebook since they require students to be specific.

- Create your own processing statements that require filling in blanks with specific words or phrases.

- Allow enough time for processing so that you do not have to accept vague responses.

- Take time to press students into being more specific. "What does a 'good job' look like and sound like?"

Students Are Not Involved. This happens when one person does the processing and all the others simply agree, or when someone does not offer any response.

Possible Remedies:

- Do processing in writing.

- Use a Processing Sheet (see Appendix F for examples).

- Each person does "I" Analysis Processing.

- Student not involved in processing is assigned to be recorder/spokesperson for the group.

- Students take turns being recorder.

- All group members sign the Processing Sheet to show participation and agreement.

Written Processing Is Not Acceptable. This happens when students either do not attempt to do processing, fail to complete the processing, or do not deliver a neat and readable finished product.

Possible Remedies:

- Include processing as part of the task (as #6 of a sheet of five problems).

- Students sign each other's Processing Sheets to show that each has been checked for neatness and completion.

- Give a reward on completeness and neatness.

Roadblock: Students Do Not Use Social Skills During Processing

This roadblock is in evidence when you hear arguing and negative comments, or when the group is not working as a team.

Possible Remedies:

- Remind groups beforehand to use social skills.

- Teacher observes and makes notes. Reports on observations before next day's processing time.

- Assign social skills during processing.

Roadblock: Students Hesitate To Give Their Own Opinions

This roadblock occurs when students give you what they think you want to hear or when they wait for your opinion rather than risk sharing theirs.

Possible Remedies:

- Begin with Fill-in-the-Blank processing; then move to more risky methods (Values Voting, Forced Choice, and Continuums).

- Wait until students have processed before giving your opinions.

- Eliminate your evaluative praise or criticism.

- Give objective feedback with occasional descriptive praise or criticism.

- Persevere! Students need time and practice to trust you and to trust their own opinions.

Signs of Success

Since processing takes much time and effort, it is important to be aware of the signs of success. You will know that processing is working when you notice *any* of the following:

- Everyone is involved in processing.

- Responses are clear and specific.

- Social skills are used during processing.

- Students give their opinions easily and candidly.

- You hear processing going on *before* and *after* processing time.

- Social skill behavior improves—in groups and elsewhere.

When you notice *most* of the behaviors above, you know that it is time to phase out formal processing. Just as you phase out assigning specific social skills, the processing can become informal, too. You might occasionally ask a question of the whole group (''What social skills were you conscious of using today?'') or ask small groups to briefly discuss social skills (''What social skills would have been helpful to use in your group today?'').

Trust that your skills, patience and effort will make processing a rewarding experience for you and your students. Even if students are reluctant, remember that you are training students in life-long skills. These skills will help your students learn from their experiences rather than repeat the same self-defeating behaviors day after day; year after year.

We have defined social skills and have outlined options for processing the use of these skills for cooperative learning. In Chapter 8, the focus will be upon positive interdependence. The positive interdependence which you structure will provide the necessary motivation for your students to learn and practice cooperative social skills. Positive interdependence is the final ingredient for building successful cooperative learning experiences.

8
Positive Interdependence

Teachers in our workshops and classes often fantasize about how much their students will enjoy working in cooperative groups. They are sure that youngsters who take every opportunity to interact in the classroom will be delighted to finally have legitimate reasons to work together. They are convinced that students will enthusiastically move into group work because working with others would appear to be more fun than working alone. Consequently, one of the biggest surprises for teachers beginning to use cooperative groups is that these fantasies are not always true. Some students want to work only in a group with their best friends. Others prefer to work alone. Still others would rather not do any work at all.

Some students prefer to work alone because they have been trained that way. Teachers have taught students to "Look at your own paper," "Don't tell anyone the answer," and that "Sharing answers is cheating." The "bad news" is that students have successfully learned to operate from such an "I, me, my" perspective. "*I* have to do *my* work at *my* desk." The "good news" is that students can be taught to adopt an "Us, we, our" stance so that during cooperative group work, words like "*We* have to finish *our* paper to get a reward for *us*," are easy to say, believe, and act out.

This re-teaching involves more than wishing students would work together or crossing our fingers hoping for a group that is willing to cooperate. More than luck, the full moon, or magic is required. It requires a conscious and continuous effort to structure reasons for students to work together. It requires *positive interdependence*.

Positive Interdependence

Positive interdependence is a term that describes the relationship between members of a cooperative group. Students in a cooperative group succeed only if every member of the group succeeds. If one fails, they all suffer. They are positively interdependent because, in order for everyone to be successful, they must care about whether or not *all* their group members are successful.

Initially, most students do not automatically care about the others in the group. For that reason, this relationship must be created by the teacher. This is why we often call positive interdependence "phony caring." It is phony because at first students care about how their groupmates operate only because it affects them. In time, however, this caring becomes sincere. Students will genuinely want their groupmates to be successful because they care about them as individuals.

When positive interdependence is in place in groups, these are typical behaviors:

- Students stay with their group.

- Students talk about the task.

- Materials are shared.

- Answers are shared.

- Students drill each other on the material.

- Others watch as one person writes.

- Heads are close together over the group's paper.

When positive interdependence is *not* in place, these behaviors are typical:

- Students leave their group without the group's permission.

- Students talk, but not about the task.

- Students protect their answers and do not share.

- No one checks to see if others have learned the material.

- Each person is writing.

- People lean back, working independently, not involved in the group effort.

Specific strategies to encourage students to "care" about their groupmates are needed to insure desired cooperative group outcomes.

Strategies For Creating Positive Interdependence

Strategic use of resources, accountability and rewards can foster positive interdependence. Such techniques will be discussed in this section.

Resource Accountability

Students are tied together through resource interdependence when they must share resources or responsibilities to complete a task. This can be done through limited resources; jigsawed materials; and/or assigned tasks.

Limited resources means that there are fewer materials than there are group members. For example, instead of three pencils for a group of three, there is only one. Instead of three identical worksheets to complete, there is one. Rulers, scissors, poster board, and dictionaries are other examples of materials that can be limited.

When each student has his or her own paper and pencil, the group looks very different from one in which there is *one* piece of paper and *one* pencil. In the former situation, everyone sits back and does his or her own work—there is little interaction. In the latter situation, group members are seen with their heads together over the paper as one person uses the pencil. Students can clearly be seen leaning into the experience and even bumping heads if they are not careful.

In some groups, having one pair of scissors, one marker, and one stapler can be the impetus for students creating a production line. We observed this in a third grade class where students decided to take a turn at each job. One cut out circles, one wrote homonyms on the circles, and one stapled the circles together. The end products were a Homonym Worm and everyone's knowledge of how to spell all of the homonyms written on the worm. As the production line flowed, there was talk of homonyms, spelling, circles, and stapling. These students demonstrated resource interdependence in action.

Samples of Resources That Can Be Limited
(fewer items than there are group members)

Pencil	Protractor
Crayons	Typewriter
Textbook	Thesaurus
Answer sheet	Sewing machine
Ruler	Fabric
Paper	Template
Scissors	Triangle
Dictionary	Glue
Map	Roll of tape
Compass	Clay
Periodic chart of elements	Basketball
Card catalog	Soccer ball

Jigsawed materials refers to dividing up the work or materials so that each group member does a part. No one has everything that is needed to complete the task. In Mr. Jordan's classroom (Chapter 2), each student received only two of the ten spelling words to study, learn and teach to the others. No one had the complete list, so group members depended on each other to obtain all ten words.

Jigsawing can also be used when students are doing research for a report. Each member of the group is assigned a part of a famous person's life, an aspect of a war, or the events leading to a discovery.* After research has been completed, the final report is put together by the group.

Another method of jigsawing is to divide an assignment so that each group member does a part. For example, if a group's assignment is to write the definitions, phonetic spellings and sentences for a list of words, the task is shared. One student writes the definitions, one provides the phonetic spellings, and one writes sentences to demonstrate understanding of the words. The next day everyone checks the work

---

*For additional ideas on jigsawing materials, see E. Aronson, *The Jigsaw Classroom* (Beverly Hills, CA: Sage, 1978).

and reaches agreement on the correct answers. Everyone in the group is responsible for knowing all parts of the assignment.

Materials can also be jigsawed for primary students. In a first grade class which we observed, three students were responsible for working together to put three pictures in chronological order. Each student had one of the pictures and all three pictures had to be used to complete the sequence. In another class, three kindergarteners were drawing a picture requiring the use of six different colored crayons. Because each student had two crayons with which only he or she could color, each person's materials were essential for completion of the product.

Samples of Materials That Can Be Jigsawed
(group members have different materials or parts of the work)

Words	Colored markers/crayons
Pictures	Resource books
Definitions	Drafting tools
Sections of report	Lab equipment
Parts of puzzle	Art supplies
Homework problems	Sewing supplies
Parts of directions	Ingredients for cooking

Assigned tasks means that no one does all the jobs necessary to complete the work. One person writes, one person reads, one person proofreads, or one person checks the dictionary for a correct spelling. This task may be assigned for the entire work period or may be shifted from person to person within the group so that everyone has a turn. The teacher decides whether to assign the tasks or let the students decide. The teacher also decides whether or not every person in the group has a specific role. It might be that there is one person who cuts, one who tapes, and one who draws; everyone has a job. Or, there might be a reader and a writer in a group, with one student not having a specific job.

Samples of Tasks That Can Be Shared

Reading	Sewing
Writing	Gluing
Proofreading	Cutting
Dictionary checking	Taping
Drawing, coloring	Stapling
Running for supplies	Dribbling
Measuring	Kicking
Map checking	Typing

Accountability Interdependence

Another way to increase the chances that students will feel bound to members of their group is to establish how each individual will be held accountable for knowing the material studied. The group succeeds when its individual members succeed.

Establishing Criteria—Before checking to see how much each group member has learned, it is necessary to decide what is required for the groups to reach criteria—that is, to perform in a satisfactory manner.

We recommend setting a criterion low enough so that every group has a chance to reach it and high enough so that each group has to work to achieve it. This might be 70-90% depending on the material and the students' familiarity with it. If you decide that reaching criterion means getting 100%, then the work should be a review of something you believe all students have learned. Some teachers find that if the criterion for satisfactory group work is consistently 100%, some groups may give up because they are unable to reach it. If the work is too easy, groups may complete the task too quickly and not feel challenged. A reasonable criterion is one that requires groups to spend sufficient time on the work and yet is possible to attain.

A criterion may be set for the group to reach, or it might be that each person in the group has her or his individual criterion. A skilled speller may have to achieve 95% on a spelling test, an average speller 85%, and a less skilled speller 70% to reach criterion. Whatever the criteria, be sure that students are informed ahead of time and that your expectations are clear.

Methods of Determining Accountability—There are three ways to determine a group's mastery of subject matter. Decide which method you will use depending upon what is comfortable for you and your students.

(1) Each individual takes a test which covers the material assigned to the group. The group's score is determined by:

- Adding individual scores together

- Taking the average of all scores

- Choosing one test to be checked as the group test

- Using the lowest test score as the group's score

- Giving the group a point for each person who reaches her or his own criterion

(2) The teacher chooses one individual in each group to answer one question about the task. The group meets the criterion and each person in the group gets credit if that one person answers correctly. No credit is given for a wrong answer.

(3) One group member is chosen by the teacher, or randomly selected, to take the test for his or her group. That person's score becomes the group's score.

It is possible to give groups that do not reach the criterion another opportunity to do so. To encourage more practice and learning, let students take the test again or have another chance to answer the question.

There are some group tasks that do not lend themselves to individual testing. These include work on murals, reports, and questions that ask for opinions. To determine whether everyone participated and agreed with the content of the mural, report, or answers, have each person sign her or his name. A signature means that ''I agree with what is here and I participated.'' If, after the product has been evaluated, someone in the group who has signed her or his name says that she or he did not agree or no one let her or him participate, a reminder of what a signature means can be reviewed. Not signing is an indication of conflict or lack of participation and is discussed during processing.

Reward Interdependence

This form of interdependence is the most powerful of the three types and also the easiest to misuse. It is powerful because group members demonstrate caring behaviors for one another and help one another learn because they want the reward. It can be misused because students tend to quickly get "hooked" on rewards and expect them in return for any work they complete. Offer rewards to your students only if they are resistant to working together. If they are willing to cooperate and offer little resistance, use the other types of interdependence strategies.

Some students may be accustomed to being rewarded when working individually or competitively. Two differences must be made clear to them before they begin.

- Each group member receives the same reward, based on how well the group and its individual members perform. It is not possible for one group member to earn 15 extra minutes of recess while the rest of the group receives only 5 minutes.

- Every group that meets the criterion receives the reward. Each group may receive a round of applause, ten bonus points on homework, or a turn to be first in line to lunch. If the reward is given to the first group which completes the task or to the group with the highest score, groups not getting the reward feel resentment toward the winners. This resentment interferes with the group's being able to figure out how they can do better next time. Also it is important to avoid such inter-group competition, because it breaks down feelings of cooperation within the classroom.

Using Reward Interdependence—If you decide to use rewards, you will want to come up with a list of rewards which is attractive to students, which is not expensive, and which contains no rewards you would find objectionable.

We recommend brainstorming with students to determine a list of rewards. Examine the list together to determine which rewards are appropriate in terms of cost, school rules, and your comfort zone. For example, if you really hate popcorn parties, scratch that one from the list. If leaving school early is against school policy, eliminate that one. (See our compiled list of rewards which other teachers have used in Appendix G.)

Although rewards must be attractive, it is important to be able to offer them more than once so that groups which do not earn the reward one time will have another opportunity. We do not want students threatening each other or attempting bodily harm because they missed the weekend in Chicago! We do want students to figure out what they can do differently next time so that they may use the new markers or lab equipment.

Dispense with the use of rewards as soon as students begin to willingly work in groups. You will know you have reached this point when students (1) request permission to do an assignment in groups, (2) ask eagerly when they will be working in groups again, or (3) start to work before you even mention rewards. It is best to eliminate rewards as soon as possible because it is more difficult to remove them after students become accustomed to receiving them. Furthermore, it is not our intention for you to constantly "pay" students for doing their work.

Groups Not Reaching Criteria—No teacher wants to see students fail. It is not easy to see a group not earn the reward, especially when all of the other groups are successful. However, it is important for groups who do not reach a criterion to deal with the consequences. If you never allow groups to fail, there are no lessons to be learned from below criteria performance.

We encourage you to set up criteria such that each group must strive to reach predetermined goals. If groups do not perform, they will miss the reward for that day. This gives groups an opportunity to problem-solve, experiment with solutions, and be successful on another occasion. Resist the impulse to rescue students from making mistakes. Making mistakes often provides a valuable learning experience. Your attempts to rescue could limit possible opportunities for important growth and development.

Goal Interdependence

Building in external reasons for students to cooperate will eventually lead to internal motivation to work in groups. Students exhibit goal interdependence when they need no rewards, motivators, or reminders about how to work in a group. When given a task to do, they do it with energy and enthusiasm. People talk to one another, receive input from everyone in the group, share ideas and create a positive rewarding experience for themselves. We call this the "Mount Everest Theory" which describes why groups work on a task when there is no reward or accountability interdependence. Just as mountain climbers explain why they want to climb Mount Everest ("just because it's there"), each group works on a task, just because it is there.

There are no guarantees as to how long it takes students to reach this stage. It could take some students just a few sessions and others a few months. Your students will grow towards goal interdependence as you give them more opportunities to work together and solve their problems independently.

Reducing Problem Behaviors Through Positive Interdependence

As you observe your students working in groups, you may have noticed some unhelpful behaviors that occur again and again. You notice that in spite of consistent processing sessions and after assigning new social skills, these behaviors continue. To help you recognize and diagnose these behaviors, we have divided the most common ones into four categories of behavior. In this section we describe these behaviors and suggest how specific strategies for creating positive interdependence can be used in each situation. If you recognize any of these behaviors as problems in your classroom, you may want to incorporate one of the suggested strategies into your next cooperative group lesson.

Passive Uninvolvement

Typical Behaviors

- Turning away from the group

- Not participating

- Not paying attention to the work

- Saying little or nothing

- Showing no enthusiasm

- Not bringing work or materials

Suggested Strategies

- Jigsaw resources so that the passively uninvolved student has materials or information the others need. Either the student will share materials or group members will include the student in order to get the needed material.

- Assign tasks and give the passively uninvolved student a job that is essential to the group's success—reader, writer, etc.

- Use accountability interdependence. Arrange for the passively uninvolved person's test score to be averaged with the others or have this individual's performance be critical to the group's success.

- Offer a reward which will motivate or encourage the passively uninvolved individual or the group to become involved.

Active Uninvolvement

Typical Behaviors

- Talking about everything but the task

- Leaving the group without the group's permission

- Attempting to sabotage the group's work by giving wrong answers or destroying the product

- Refusing to work with someone in the group

Suggested Strategies

- Structure accountability interdependence by offering a reward that this individual or group finds attractive. Tie it to a test or checking system so that the actively uninvolved person must cooperate in order for the group to succeed and get the reward.

Independence of Groupmates

Typical Behaviors

- Uninvolvement with the group

- Doing work alone

- Ignoring group discussion

Suggested Strategies

- Jigsaw materials so that the independent student cannot do the work without obtaining materials from the other students. To accomplish the task, the individual must interact and cooperate.

- Limit resources. If there is only one answer sheet and pencil, this person is unable to do the work alone.

Taking Charge of Groupmates

Typical Behaviors

- Doing all the work

- Refusing to let others help

- Ordering others around

- Bullying group members

- Making decisions without checking for agreement

Suggested Strategies

- Jigsaw resources so that this person must cooperate with others to obtain the needed materials or information.

- Assign tasks giving others in the group the most powerful jobs like reader, writer, checker, etc.

- Use reward and accountability interdependence. If everyone has to take an individual test and meet criteria to get the reward, group members are likely to take their turns and not allow one individual to assume total responsibility for completing the task.

Conclusion

At this point you and your students have identified and learned specific social skills necessary for cooperative learning. Processing sessions help groups to refine and assimilate these social skills. Positive interdependence techniques provide motivation for students to work effectively in groups. You may be wondering when you may safely begin phasing out the formal teaching of cooperation. You will know your students are able to work cooperatively with a minimum of teacher direction when:

- You see students in a tight circle working on the assigned task

- You notice a formerly negative student encouraging a groupmate

- You hear students setting goals for which social skill they will use more consistently next time

As you notice your students frequently and spontaneously demonstrating such skills of cooperation, you will know that all the weeks of time and energy have been well invested. You will know that you and your students have reached your goal: effective learning in a cooperative school climate.

Appendix A
Cooperative Learning Lesson Plan Worksheet

Name _____   Grade_____

System _____   Bldg. _____

Subject _____   # of students_____

Directions: Check one or more items in each category, unless otherwise indicated. Fill in appropriate
blanks.

STEP 1. Lesson

A. Outcome of the Lesson (general goal):

☐ to memorize_____

☐ to practice _____

B. Subject Matter Task (specific objective): State in language your students will understand.

"Your *group* will work cooperatively to:

1. _____   4. _____

2. _____   5. _____

3. _____   6. _____"

C. Learning Experience(s) That Precede Group Work:

☐ lecture on_____

☐ homework assignment on _____

☐ lesson on _____

D. Time for this *one* session is ____ minutes (includes directions, work time, and processing).

STEP 2. Group Composition And Room Arrangement

A. Group Size: _3_

B. Teacher-Selected Heterogeneous Groups. Criteria for Selection: (Choose 1 or 2)

☐ High/average/low skills in _____

☐ Handicapped/nonhandicapped

☐ Male/female

☐ Racial

☐ Outgoing/shy

☐ _____

C. Physical Setting for Students:
(Close enough so all can see and hear; on same level; space between groups)

☐ _____ chairs in a circle

☐ _____ students on floor in circle

☐ _____ desks with _____ chairs

STEP 3. Positive Interdependence (The ''We sink or swim together'' feeling; phony caring)
(Choose one in A; may choose B and/or C)

A. Resource Interdependence

☐ Jigsawed (each group member has a different part of the work or materials)

☐ Limited (each group gets fewer materials than there are group members)

Materials

Number Needed: Description:

_____   _____

_____   _____

_____   _____

☐ B. Accountability Interdependence (teacher evaluation of group work):

☐ explanation of group's work from individual(s)

☐ check the group's paper

☐ individual test to each student

Criteria (standard for judgment)

☐ grades

☐ percents

___ = _____   ___ = _____

___ = _____   ___ = _____

___ = _____

☐ C. Reward Interdependence (each person in the group gets the same one;
reward is available to all groups):

☐ Group recognition of _____

☐ Special privilege of _____

☐ A tangible reward of _____

STEP 4. Social Skills
(Choose 1 or 2) Teacher Uses Observation Sheet

Task: ☐ Check for understanding

☐ Share ideas and information

Maintenance: ☐ Encourage

☐ Check for agreement

STEP 5. Processing

A. Subject Matter (Choose 1):

☐ Some ways we checked our facts are _____,

_____, and _____.

☐ One way we memorized _____ was to

_____ .

☐ We practiced _____ by _____ .

B. Social Skills (Choose *one* type and *one* method)

☐ Analysis (examination of this group experience)

   ☐ Our group did well on _____

                                   (social skill)

     by _____ , _____ , and _____ .

          (three behaviors)

   ☐ Continuums _____

            Always   Never

We checked for understanding.

We shared ideas and information.

We encouraged each other to participate.

We checked for agreement.

☐ Application (transfer of social skill learnings to other situations)

   ☐ We learned that in any group it is helpful to _____

     _____ .

   ☐ The social skill of _____ could be used at other

     times like _____ .

☐ Goal Setting (plans for next group session with same group members)

   ☐ The social skill we will use more next time is _____

     because _____ .

   ☐ The social skill we will practice more next time is _____

     by _____ , _____

          (three behaviors)

     and _____ .

C.   Format (how processing will be done)

   1. ☐ written

       ☐ oral

   2. ☐ individual

       ☐ groups

Form B-1

Appendix B
Beginning Observation Forms

Names

Skills

Form B-2

Lesson: _____   Date: _____

Group #	Names	Social Skills		
		1. _____	2. _____	3. _____

Appendix C
Non-Academic Cooperative Learning Activities

Art projects

    bulletin boards
    construction projects
    display cases
    murals

Class float

Class play

    pick cast
    complete set
    advertise

Clean-up

    athletic field
    auditorium
    gym
    lab
    room
    school yard

Create room rules

Discussions after:

    assembly
    concert
    field trip
    record
    visitor

After discussions:

    draw pictures
    3 new things learned
    new endings

FFA, FHA

    rules and regulations
    projects

Fundraising

Holiday activities

Holiday traditions

Organize class work patterns

Prom preparation

Puzzles

    crossword
    seek-and-find
    dot-to-dot

Safety rules

    bike
    Halloween
    sports
    shop equipment
    auto

Scouts

Student Council Committees

Appendix D
Anecdotal and Informal Observation Forms

Form D-1 Assigned Skills

Directions: In the left-hand vertical column, write each group member's name. In the two horizontal slots, write the assigned social skills. When you see or hear a student practicing one of the skills, write the gesture or words opposite that student's name in the appropriate column.

Skills				
Names	Verbal	Non-Verbal	Verbal	Non-Verbal

Form D-2 Without Assigned Skills

Directions: In the left-hand vertical column, write each group member's name. When you see or hear a student practicing a helpful or non-helpful behavior, write the gesture or words opposite the student's name in the appropriate column.

	Helpful Behaviors		Unhelpful Behaviors	
Names	Verbal	Non-Verbal	Verbal	Non-Verbal

Form D-3 Informal Observation

Directions: When observing the whole class in their various groups, write the skill titles in the left-hand column and the behaviors you notice in the right-hand column.

Social Skills	Behaviors

Appendix E
Examples of Processing Statements

(See Chapter 7 for directions)

Analysis Processing

About Self

Fill in the Blank/Finish the Sentence

   1. The social skill I used most consistently today is _____

      by _____ , _____ , and _____ .
           (three specific behaviors)

   2. A social skill I enjoyed practicing today was _____

      because _____ .

   3. When someone in my group was not contributing, I _____

      _____ .

Statements to use with Forced Choice, Values Voting, or Continuums:
  (use social skills assigned in today's lesson)

     I encouraged others.
     I followed directions.
     I responded to others' ideas.
     I helped others in my group to understand the work.
     I used names.
     I asked questions when I didn't understand something.

About Others

(Fill in the Blank/Finish the Sentence)

   1. Someone who took turns was _____ .
                                  (name)

   2. The most helpful thing someone did in our group on social skills was_____

      _____ .

   3. I really felt good when others in my group _____

      _____ .

4. _____ , I enjoyed it when you_____
   (name)

   _____ .

Statements to use with Forced Choice, Values Voting, or Continuums:
(use social skills assigned in today's lesson)

> My ideas were responded to even if they were not agreed with or used.
> Others looked at me when I was talking.
> I felt encouraged in my group today.
> Others in the group helped me when I had a question.
> Others shared their materials with me.

About Us

Fill in the Blank/Finish the Sentence

1. Our group did well on _____ by _____ ,
                              (social skill)   (three specific behaviors)

   _____ ,and _____ .

2. The words we used to _____ were _____ .
                              (social skill)

                                                    _____ .

                                                    _____ .
                                                          (specific words)

3. A social skill we enjoyed practicing today was _____

   because _____ .

4. We could do better on _____ by _____ .
                              (social skill)

5. Today we really needed someone in our group to _____ .

6. The social skill we used the least was _____

   because _____ .

7. We checked for agreement (reached consensus, etc.) by _____ ,

   _____ , and_____ .
   (three specific behaviors)

Statements to use with Forced Choice, Values Voting, or Continuums:
(use social skills assigned in today's lesson)

Today as a group *we*:
accomplished our goal   disagreed in a nice way
helped each other   accepted each others' ideas
felt good about working together   took turns
kept each other and ourselves on task

Application Processing

About Individual or Group

1. One thing {I   learned or relearned about group work is _____ .
             {we

2. {I   learned the following ways to _____ : _____ ,
   {We   (social skill)   (three specific behaviors)
   _____ , and _____ .

3. {I   learned that in any group it is helpful to_____ .
   {We

(The following can be responded to individually or by the group as a whole.)

4. The social skill we used that can be transferred to any group is_____ .

5. The social skill of _____ could be used at other times like

   _____ .

6. Sometimes it's better for three people to solve a problem rather than one because_____

   _____ .

7. It is important to _____ in other places besides the classroom
                         (social skill)

   because _____ .

Goal Setting Processing

About Individual or Group

1. One social skill {I   will practice more consistently next time is _____ .
                    {we

   {I   will do this by _____ , _____ , and _____ .
   {We   (three specific behaviors)

2. The social skill $\begin{cases} \text{I} \\ \text{we} \end{cases}$ want to be sure to use next time is _____

   because _____ .

3. Our group will _____ next time we meet in a group by _____
                            (social skill)

   _____ .
      (specific behavior)

Sample Processing Sheets

Primary

Use statements that deal with the assigned social skills. Statements are read aloud to the class. Each student completes the Processing Sheet by putting an X over the happy face for YES or an X over the sad face for NO. When each group has reached consensus, the teacher writes in the goal setting answer.

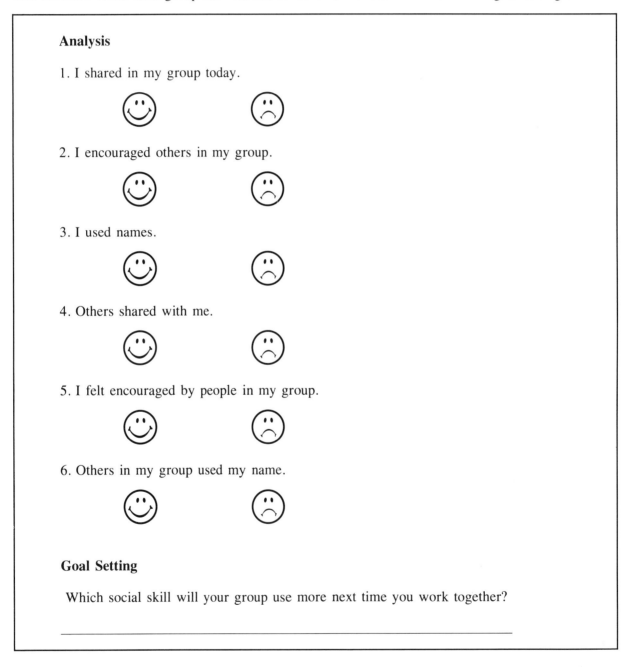

Analysis

1. I shared in my group today.

2. I encouraged others in my group.

3. I used names.

4. Others shared with me.

5. I felt encouraged by people in my group.

6. Others in my group used my name.

Goal Setting

Which social skill will your group use more next time you work together?

_____

Upper Elementary/Junior High

Analysis

Put an X on the line where you think you or your group performed on social skills in today's lesson.

1. I encouraged others.

   _____
   ALWAYS   NEVER

2. I followed directions.

   _____
   ALWAYS   NEVER

3. I responded to others' ideas.

   _____
   ALWAYS   NEVER

4. We encouraged everyone in our group.

   _____
   ALWAYS   NEVER

5. We followed directions.

   _____
   ALWAYS   NEVER

6. We responded to others' ideas.

   _____
   ALWAYS   NEVER

Goal Setting

Fill in the blanks with a word or phrase that you feel best completes the sentence.

The social skill I will practice more consistently next time is _____

_____ . I will do this by _____ ,
                                                  (three specific behaviors)

_____ , and _____ .

Senior High/Adult

Analysis

Fill in the blanks with a word or phrase that you feel best completes the sentence.

The social skill we used most consistently today is _____

by_____ ,_____ , and
       (three specific behaviors)

_____ .

_____ , I appreciate the way you helped our group today by
  (name)

_____ .
(specific behavior)

Goal Setting

The social skill we want to be sure to use next time is _____

because_____

_____ .

Appendix G

Rewards

For Elementary School Students

Recognition

Happy Gram
  to student
  to parent
  to principal
Students of the week
Recognition in daily
  announcements
Smile
Pat on back
Hug
Display work
Standing ovation
Round of applause
Encouraging words

Privileges

Library pass
Free time
Extra recess
Stay in at recess
Silent reading time
Help other students or
  teachers in building
Help teacher with project
Choose the day's story
Helper for the day
  Pass out papers
  Run errands
  Water plants, etc.
Extra Art
Extra PE
Extra Music
Choose where to sit
Work in hall
Line up first for:
  Recess
  Drinks
  Go home
  Lunch
Use playground equipment
Choose class game
Lunch in room with teacher
Gum chewing
Early to lunch on special
  day
Choice of music
No assignment
Skip test or grade on
  assignment
Play with special game
  or toy
Use new markers, special
  paper, easel, etc.
Use clay, paint, etc.
Go outside for class session
Special day if all groups
  in class succeed:
  Joke Day
  Hat Day
  Stuffed Animal Day

Tangible Rewards

Stars
Stickers
Stamps
Snacks/soft drinks in room
Grab bag
Points earned toward a prize
Popcorn party
Pencil top
Eraser
Pencil
Bookmark
Tokens
AV treat
Bonus points
Extra credit
Grade

For Middle School Students

Recognition

Happy Gram
  to student
  to parent
  to principal
Students of the week
Recognition in daily
  announcements
Smile
Pat on back
Display work
Standing ovation
Round of applause
Encouraging words

Privileges

Library pass
Free time
Help other students or
  teachers in building
Help teacher with project
Choice of where to sit
Work in hall
Line up first
Gum chewing
Computer time
Early to lunch on
  special day
Choice of music
Allow to do special
  experiment
No assignment
Skip test or grade on
  assignment
No weekend homework
Go outside for class session
Special day if all groups
  in class succeed:
  Joke Day
  50's Day
  Hat Day
Play special game
Use new markers,
  special paper, easel,
  etc.
Use lab equipment
Computer time

Tangible Rewards

Snacks/soft drinks
  in room
Points earned toward
  a prize
Popcorn party
Tokens
Free pass to athletic
  event or dance
AV treat
Grade
Bonus points
Extra credit
Video game tokens

For High School Students

Recognition	Privileges	Tangible Rewards

Happy Gram
   to student
   to parent
Recognition in daily
   announcements
Smile
Pat on back
Display work
Standing ovation
Round of applause
Encouraging words
	Library pass
	Free time
	Choice of where to sit
	Use lab equipment
	Gum chewing
	Computer time
	No assignment
	Skip test
	Allow to do special experiment
	No weekend homework
	Go outside for class session
	Early to lunch on special day
	Choice of music
		Snacks/soft drinks in room
		Free pass to athletic event
		   or dance
		AV treat
		Grade
		Bonus points
		Extra credit
		Video game tokens

Appendix H
Lesson Plans

Seven sample lesson plans are included as guides to help you be creative about the lessons you can teach using cooperative groups. As you look over each of these suggested plans, consider the basic skills or concepts which you teach that could be implemented using the particular lesson plan. The reading comprehension lesson, for example, can be adopted to any content area that requires reading, such as chemistry and social studies. Keep in mind the specific materials that you have available and the curriculum that you cover with your students.

You will notice that this lesson plan form is different from the beginning lesson plan form suggested in Chapter 3. This is to give you more flexibility in the areas of group size, number of sessions, how to choose group members, which social skills to assign, and which processing questions to ask. Use the chapters in the Beyond Beginning section to help you make decisions about these areas.

Cooperative Learning
Lesson Plan Worksheet

Subject: *any matching*

Grade levels: *K-2*

STEP 1. Lesson

A. Outcome of the lesson:

Students will practice the skill of matching

B. Subject Matter Task:

"Your group will work cooperatively to:

1. Match (choose one per lesson):

- *colors*

- *numerals with objects*

- *shapes with names*

- *words with objects*

- *pictures of objects with beginning sounds*

2. Make sure everyone in your group can do the matching."

C. Learning Experience(s) that precede group work:

Students receive instruction for pre-requisite matching skills.

D. Length and # of sessions: *20* minutes *1* session(s)

STEP 2. Group Composition and Room Arrangement

    A.   Group size: *3*

    B.   Assignment to groups: (check one)

        ☐ Random   Method _____

        ☒ Teacher-selected   Criteria: *boys and girls*
                                                            outgoing/shy

    C.   Room arrangement: *students will sit in circles on the floor with space between groups*

STEP 3. Positive Interdependence

	Materials: # Needed	Description
A. Resource interdependence:	*1 set per group*	*flash cards/pictures*
☐ Jigsawed		*color cards/shapes*
☒ Limited		

    B.   Accountability Interdependence:

        • *Sign for agreement*

        • *Each person in the group will correctly respond to a flash card,*

         picture, shape, etc.

        Criteria: *none*

    C.   Reward Interdependence: *Each successful group will sit with*

                           the teacher at lunch in the cafeteria.

STEP 4. Social Skills Task

Social Skills: *Encourage*

Check for agreement

Type of observation form: *objective—group form*

STEP 5. Processing

A. Subject Matter: One way we remembered our

was by

B. Social Skills:

X Analysis: *We checked for agreement:*   a lot   some   none

X Application: *We could encourage at other times like*

☐ Goal Setting:

C. Format

1. ☐ Written

   X Oral

   ☐ Individual

   X Groups

Cooperative Learning
Lesson Plan Worksheet

Subject: <u>Writing—Proofreading</u>

_____

Grades: <u>3-12</u> _____

STEP 1. Lesson

A. Outcome of the lesson:

Students will correctly punctuate ten sentences* _____

_____

B. Subject Matter Task:

"Your group will work cooperatively to: _____

1. Correctly punctuate ten sentences. _____

2. Read each sentence. _____

3. Apply the rules we have studied for punctuation. _____

4. Add all punctuation that is necessary. _____

5. Each group member is to agree to all punctuation that is necessary. _____

6. Each group member is to agree to all punctuation which is added." _____

C. Learning Experience(s) that precede group work:

Students will have completed whole class and individual work on punctuation. _____

D. Length and # of sessions: <u>40</u> minutes   <u>1</u> session(s)

STEP 2. Group Composition And Room Arrangement

A. Group size: <u>4</u>

*This same lesson can be completed by a cooperative group using a micro-computer. Students will need a word processing program and editing skills with use of the machine.

To the task statement add: Every group member will discuss and agree how the microcomputer will be used to make any corrections.

B. Assignment to groups: (Check one)

        ☒ Random   Method   *One each whose birthday is in*

                                                1) winter, 2) spring, 3) summer,

                                                4) fall.

        ☐ Teacher-selected   Criteria: _____

C. Desk and room arrangement: *Students sit in chairs around one desk.*

STEP 3. Positive Interdependence

	Materials: # Needed	Description

A.   Resource Interdependence:

	1	*paper with sentences*

☐ Jigsawed   *1*   *pencil or pen*

☒ Limited

B.   Accountability Interdependence: *After completing the worksheet, students will separate from their group. Each student will be given one of the ten sentences from the worksheet to correctly punctuate on his or her own. The scores of all four completed sentences will be combined to make the group grade.*

Criteria: *90-100% = A*   *90-100% = 20 minutes*

           80-89 = B   *80-89 = 15 minutes*

           70-79 = C   *70-79 = 10 minutes*

           60-69 = D   *0-69 = no minutes*

           0-59 = E

C.   Reward Interdependence: *70% and above = time on computer for a game*

STEP 4. Social Skills Task

Social Skills: *Seek information and opinions* _____

Use names _____

_____

Type of observation form: *anecdotal* _____

STEP 5. Processing

A.   Subject Matter: *The most difficult part of our assignment was* _____

_____

B.   Social Skills:

☒ Analysis: *Our group did well on seeking information and opinions by* _____

_____ , _____ , *and*

_____ .

☒ Application: *One thing we learned or relearned about using names was* _____

_____

☐ Goal Setting: _____

_____

C.   Format:

1.   ☐ Written

☒ Oral

2 .   ☐ Individual

☒ Groups

Cooperative Learning
Lesson Plan Worksheet

Subject: *Reading Comprehension*

(all content areas)

Grades: *2-12*

STEP 1. Lesson

    A.   Outcome of the lesson:

       Students will complete six comprehension questions which refer to their reading of a

       story/chapter/paragraph

    B.   Subject Matter Task:

       ''Your group will work cooperatively to: *complete the six comprehension questions.*

       1) The group members will give their two homework responses to the group.

       2) As each question is read, the group will add two more possible answers to the one

       given response.

       3) The group will then reach consensus as to the best of the three responses for each of

       the six questions.''

    C.   Learning Experience(s) that precede group work:

       All group members will have read the story/chapter/paragraph for homework and have

       chosen one response to each of their two assigned questions.

    D.   Length and # of sessions: *60* minutes   *1* session(s)

STEP 2. Group Composition and Room Arrangement

    A.   Group size: *3*

    B.   Assignment to groups: (check one)

            ☐ Random   Method   _____

            ☒ Teacher-selected   Criteria: *shy and outgoing students*

                                                          mixed in each group

    C.   Desk and room arrangement: *Students will sit in a circle of chairs.*

STEP 3. Positive Interdependence

		Materials: # Needed	Description
A.	Resource Interdependence:	*1*	*completed paper per group*
	☒ Jigsawed	*2*	*assigned questions*
	☒ Limited	*1*	*book/chapter/paragraph*

B. Accountability Interdependence: *1) Before the group convenes, the teacher will check to see that each person's homework is complete. 10 bonus points will be added to the group score if all group members have completed homework.*

2) All students will sign the completed paper to show agreement with the answers.

Criteria: *Credit will be given if all six questions have three responses with the best one chosen as an answer.*

C. Reward Interdependence: _____

STEP 4. Social Skills Task

Social Skills: *Respond to ideas*

Disagree in an agreeable way

_____

Type of observation form: *none*

STEP 5. Processing

A. Subject Matter: *One way we reached agreement on our answers was* _____ .

B. Social Skills:

    ☒ Analysis: *I felt responded to when* _____ *said* _____

_____ .

    ☒ Application: *One method I used to disagree in an agreeable way was to* _____

_____ .

    ☐ Goal Setting: _____

_____

C. Format

    1 . ☒ Written

       ☐ Oral

    2 . ☒ Individual

       ☐ Groups

Cooperative Learning
Lesson Plan Worksheet

Subject: *Math*

Grade levels: *3-12*

STEP 1. Lesson

A. Outcome of the lesson:

Students will complete six story problems.

B. Subject Matter Task:

"Your group will work cooperatively to:

1. read and solve each story problem, and

2. be prepared to explain how each problem was completed."

C. Learning Experience(s) that precede group work:

Students will have completed whole class and individual work dealing with specific content; i.e., area; volume; fractions; etc.

D. Length and # of sessions: *55* minutes   *1* session(s)

STEP 2. Group Composition and Room Arrangement

A. Group size: *5*

B. Assignment to groups: (Check one)

☒ Random   Method *Count off by (Divide total # in class by 5 to determine # of groups and counting # as well)*

☐ Teacher-selected   Criteria:

C. Desk and room arrangement: *Chairs around both ends of each long table*

STEP 3. Positive Interdependence

		Materials: # Needed	Description
A.	Resource Interdependence:	*1*	*paper with story problems*
	☐ Jigsawed	*1*	*answer sheet*
	☒ Limited	*1*	*pen or pencil*

B. Accountability Interdependence: *Sign to show agreement.*

One person who is chosen by the teacher from each group will be asked to explain how one

of the six problems was solved.

Criteria: _____   _____

                _____   _____

                _____   _____

C. Reward Interdependence: *A holiday sticker for each group member of each successful group.*

STEP 4. Social Skills Task

Social Skills: *Share opinions*

                   Check for understanding

Type of observation form: *objective—whole class*

STEP 5. Processing

A. Subject Matter: *The easiest problem to solve was #*   *because*

B. Social Skills:

   ☒ Analysis: *I felt checked when*   *asked me*

     to

[X] Application: *I learned that in any group it is helpful to* _____

_____

[ ] Goal Setting: _____

_____

C. Format

1. [ ] Written

   [X] Oral

2. [X] Individual

   [ ] Groups

**Cooperative Learning
Lesson Plan Worksheet**

Subject: *Social Interactions*

(all content areas)

Grades: *4-9*

STEP 1. Lesson

A.   Outcome of the lesson:

To learn names of everyone in the group, alphabetize names, and discover two hobbies of each

of the group members.

B.   Subject Matter Task:

"Your group will work cooperatively to:

1. learn names of everyone in the group,

2. write them down,

3. alphabetize them,

4. learn two hobbies each person in group is interested in.

5. You will hand in the paper with names alphabetized,

6. then each person will introduce someone in the group to the class

   and share one of his or her hobbies."

C.   Learning experience(s) that precede group work: *Knowledge of alphabetizing by majority of*

the group (prerequisite)

D.   Length and # of sessions: *45* minutes   *1* session(s)

STEP 2. Group Composition and Room Arrangement

A.   Group size: *5*

B.   Assignment to groups: (Check one)

☐   Random   Method_____

B.   ☒ Teacher-selected   Criteria: *boys/girls*

Knowledge of alphabetizing/little knowledge

of alphabetizing

Isolates in separate groups

C.   Desk and room arrangement: *Circles of chairs; students on floor in circles*

STEP 3. Positive Interdependence

A.   Resource Interdependence:

	Materials: # Needed	Description
☐ Jigsawed	*1*	*piece of paper*
☒ Limited	*1*	*pencil*

B.   Accountability Interdependence: _____

One person in each group will be asked to name everyone in his or her group and 2 hobbies.

Criteria: *Must get name right and at least one of his/her hobbies.*

C.   Reward Interdependence: *Smelly stickers for each person in group of each successful group.*

STEP 4. Social Skills Task

Social Skills: *Use names*

Encourage

Check for agreement

Type of observation form: *Objective-group form*

STEP 5. Processing

A.   Subject Matter: *A hobby that sounds like fun is*

B.   Social Skills:

    ☒ Analysis: *Our group did well on* _____ *by* _____

                                                       (social skill)

    _____ , _____ *and* _____

               (specific behaviors)

    _____ .

    ☒ Application: *One thing we learned about group work is* _____ ____

    _____

    ☐ Goal Setting: _____

    _____

C.   Format

     1.   ☐ Written

         ☒ Oral

     2.   ☐ Individual

         ☒ Groups

Cooperative Learning
Lesson Plan Worksheet

Subject: *Science/Biology*

_____

Grades: *4-12*

STEP 1. Lesson

    A.   Outcome of the lesson:

        Students will label major bones in the human skeleton.

    B.   Subject Matter Task:

        "Your group will work cooperatively to label all bones that are shown on your worksheet

        skeleton (or in laboratory manual). Each group member is to agree to the name and

        spelling of each bone labeled."

    C.   Learning Experience(s) that precede group work:

        lecture on bones and functions, viewing of skeleton model

    D.   Length and # of sessions: *40* minutes   *1* session(s)

STEP 2. Group Composition and Room Arrangement

    A.   Group size: *3*

    B.   Assignment to groups: (Check one)

        ☐ Random   Method

        ☒ Teacher-selected   Criteria: *mixed academic abilities*

                                          males and females

C.   Desk and room arrangement: *Students will sit in chairs at small tables (or on stools at*

one end of laboratory tables)

STEP 3. Positive Interdependence

	Materials: # Needed	Description
A. Resource Interdependence:	*1*	*Skeleton worksheet*
☐ Jigsawed	*1*	*pencil or pen*
☒ Limited		

B.   Accountability Interdependence: *Students will sign worksheet to show*

agreement.

Criteria: *75% or more correct labels = passing and reward*

74% or less correct labels = paper must be done again

C.   Reward Interdependence: *10 bonus points per successful group*

STEP 4. Social Skills Task

Social Skills: *Share information*

Check for agreement

Type of observation form: *objective—group form*

STEP 5. Processing

    A.   Subject Matter: *One way we checked the spelling of our bones was* _____

_____

    B.   Social Skills:

        ☒ Analysis: *The words we used to check for agreement were* _____

_____ , _____ , *and*

_____

        ☒ Application: *Sharing information is a social skill that can be used at other times like*

_____

        ☐ Goal Setting: _____

_____

    C.   Format

        1. ☐ Written

            ☒ Oral

            ☐ Individual

            ☒ Groups

Cooperative Learning
Lesson Plan Worksheet

Subject: *Social Studies*

Decision Making

Grade levels: *3-12*

STEP 1. Lesson

A. Outcome of the lesson:

Students will complete a group simulation game using a

microcomputer.

B. Subject Matter Task:

"Your group will work cooperatively to:

*1. complete your share of the 'dig' in the computer game Archaeology Search.**

2. Everyone in the group is to agree on the decisions made and

3. agree how the computer keyboard will be used to select and

   complete your decisions.

4. Your group will share your information with other groups so

   that the classroom 'dig' is a success.''

C. Learning Experience(s) that precede group work:

lecture and discussion regarding archaeology and use of microcomputer (pre-requisite)

D. Length and # of sessions: *15* minutes   *4* session(s)

*"Archaeology Search," Webster Division McGraw-Hill. Some other group simulation games which you might wish to use include Oregon Trail (Minnesota Educational Computing Consortium); Lemonade Stand (Commodore Public Domain); and Pizza Stand (Commodore Public Domain). These programs are appropriate for Grades 3-12.

STEP 2. Group Composition and Room Arrangement

A.   Group size: *2*

B.   Assignment to groups: (Check one)

        ☒ Random   Method *Pick #'s from hat which correspond to*

                                                              machine # in computer laboratory

        ☐ Teacher-Selected   Criteria: _____

C.   Desk and room arrangement: *2 chairs placed in front of each microcomputer*

STEP 3. Positive Interdependence

		Materials: # Needed	Description
A.	Resource Interdependence:	*1*	*micro per group*
	☐ Jigsawed	*1*	*disc per group*
	☒ Limited		

B.   Accountability Interdependence: *Continue to receive program money to finish the game*

     Criteria: *none*

C.   Reward Interdependence: *none*

STEP 4. Social Skills Task

Social Skills: *Share information and opinions*

Respond to ideas

Type of observation form: *none*

STEP 5. Processing

A.   Subject Matter: *One way we helped our class succeed was to*

B.   Social Skills:

Day 1, 2, 3, & 4

☒   Analysis: *The social skill we used well today was*

_____ *by* _____ , _____ , *and*

_____ .

(three behaviors)

Day 4

☒   Application: *It's important to use social skills at the microcomputer because*

_____

_____ .

Day 1, 2, 3

☒   Goal Setting: *Tomorrow we will be sure to use the social skill of*

because

_____ .

C. Format

    1. ☒ Written

        ☐ Oral

    2. ☐ Individual

        ☒ Groups

Bibliography

Aronson, E., N. Blaney, C. Stephan, J. Sikes, and M. Snapp, *The Jigsaw Classroom*. Beverly Hills, CA: Sage, 1978.

Brookover, Wilbur, B., L. Beamer, H. Efthim, D. Hathaway, L. Lezotte, S. Miller, J. Passalacqua, and L. Tornatzky, *Creating Effective Schools*. Holmes Beach, FL: Learning Publications, Inc., 1982.

Chasnoff, R. (Ed.), *Structuring Cooperative Learning: The 1979 Handbook*. Minneapolis, MN: Cooperative Network, 1979.

Clark, Jean Illsley, *We: Newsletter for Nurturing Support Groups*. 16535 9th Ave. N., Plymouth, MN 55447.

Costa, Arthur L., *The Enabling Behaviors*. San Anselmo, CA: Search Models Unlimited, 1983.

Ginott, Haim, *Between Teacher and Child*. New York, NY: The Macmillan Co., 1972.

Johnson, D.W., *Reaching Out: Interpersonal Effectiveness and Self-Actualization*. Englewood Cliffs, NJ: Prentice-Hall, 1972.

Johnson, D.W., and R. Johnson, *Joining Together: Group Therapy and Group Skills*. Englewood Cliffs, NJ: Prentice-Hall, 1975.

Johnson, D.W., and R. Johnson, *Learning Together and Alone: Cooperation, Competition, and Individualization*. Englewood Cliffs, NJ: Prentice-Hall, 1975.

Lyons, Virginia (Ed.), *Structuring Cooperative Learning: The 1980 Handbook*. Minneapolis, MN: Cooperative Network, 1980.

Moorman, Chick, and Dee Dishon, *Our Classroom: We Can Learn Together*. Englewood Cliffs, NJ: Prentice-Hall, 1983.

Roy, Patricia (Ed.), *Structuring Cooperative Learning: The 1982 Handbook*. Minneapolis, MN: Cooperative Network, 1982.

Stanford, Gene, *Developing Effective Classroom Groups*. New York, NY: Hart Publishing Co., 1977.

Stocking, S. Holly, Diana Arezzo, and Shelley Leavitt, *Helping Kids Make Friends*. Allen, TX: Argus Communications, 1979.

Index